Hands-On DevOps with Vagrant

Implement end-to-end DevOps and infrastructure
management using Vagrant

Alex Braunton

BIRMINGHAM - MUMBAI

Hands-On DevOps with Vagrant

Commissioning Editor: Gebin George
Acquisition Editor: Rohit Rajkumar
Content Development Editor: Dattatraya More
Technical Editor: Sayali Thanekar, Cymon Pereira, Nirbhaya Shaji
Copy Editor: Safis Editing
Project Coordinator: Kinjal Bari
Proofreader: Safis Editing
Indexer: Priyanka Dhadke
Graphics: Jisha Chirayil
Production Coordinator: Jyoti Chauhan

First published: October 2018

Production reference: 2061118

Published by Packt Publishing Ltd.
Livery Place
35 Livery Street
Birmingham
B3 2PB, UK.

ISBN 978-1-78913-805-4

www.packtpub.com

To my beautiful wife, Francesca,
and wonderful daughter, Florence;
without you both,
I would be nothing.
Thank you.

– Alex Braunton

`mapt.io`

Mapt is an online digital library that gives you full access to over 5,000 books and videos, as well as industry leading tools to help you plan your personal development and advance your career. For more information, please visit our website.

Why subscribe?

- Spend less time learning and more time coding with practical eBooks and Videos from over 4,000 industry professionals

- Improve your learning with Skill Plans built especially for you

- Get a free eBook or video every month

- Mapt is fully searchable

- Copy and paste, print, and bookmark content

Packt.com

Did you know that Packt offers eBook versions of every book published, with PDF and ePub files available? You can upgrade to the eBook version at `www.packt.com` and as a print book customer, you are entitled to a discount on the eBook copy. Get in touch with us at `customercare@packtpub.com` for more details.

At `www.packt.com`, you can also read a collection of free technical articles, sign up for a range of free newsletters, and receive exclusive discounts and offers on Packt books and eBooks.

Contributors

About the author

Alex Braunton is a web developer focusing on the LAMP stack by day and a technical tinkerer by night. He is passionate about all technological things and enjoys trying to build robots and home automation systems with his Raspberry Pi collection. Currently, he is focusing on sharpening his DevOps knowledge and experimenting with a range of technologies, such as serverless, virtual reality, and GraphQL. He also has a growing bonsai collection and constantly bores his wife and family about the art and history of bonsai.

I'd like to start by thanking my wife, Francesca. Without her support, this book would not have been possible.
I'd like to thank the incredible team at Packt, who have guided me along every step of this book and have been excellent - especially Rohit Rajkumar and Dattatraya More.
I'd like to thank Mitchell Hashimoto/HashiCorp for creating such a fantastic piece of software, Vagrant. Your ideas and code have truly inspired me.

About the reviewer

Michał Wołonkiewicz started by participating in the home meteo station network (involving an unbreakable DS1820 connected by a 1-Wire converter to an RS-232 interface in an Optiplex G1, operating under the control of OpenBSD) before he even got his driving license. He gained his first commercial experience as a systems engineer in both the public and private sectors, he improved the infrastructure at an investment bank and taught developers how to use it. He runs a consulting company with the goal of providing expertise on IT, Telco, and security technologies. He can be reached at michal@wolonkiewi.cz.

Special thanks to my family – my wife, Ada, and my son, Wojciech – thanks to whom I am stronger and more persistent every day.

Packt is searching for authors like you

If you're interested in becoming an author for Packt, please visit authors.packtpub.com and apply today. We have worked with thousands of developers and tech professionals, just like you, to help them share their insight with the global tech community. You can make a general application, apply for a specific hot topic that we are recruiting an author for, or submit your own idea.

Table of Contents

Preface

Vagrant is an open source tool that allows you to programatically create and manage virtual environments. Vagrant's main focus is on creating development environments that can be shared between teams all over the world. It removes the "works fine on my machine" problem and allows anyone with the Vagrantfile configuration to create an exact copy of the original machine.

Vagrant was created and is maintained by Mitchell Hashimoto and HashiCorp with a continuous stream of support and updates. It's a piece of software that has been going from strength to strength since its creation in 2010.

Who this book is for

In this book, we'll cover many aspects of Vagrant. The book can be used by beginners who have very little or no experience with Vagrant. We'll cover how to install Vagrant and all of the basic knowledge needed to get up and running.

This book can also be used by more advanced users who wish to better understand and utilize Vagrant. We'll cover the available commands, networking, multi-machine, and provisioning with configuration management tools such as Chef and Ansible.

Whatever level you are at, this book will teach you something new or help reinforce your knowledge and offer tips and tricks.

What this book covers

Chapter 1, *Introduction*, acts as a great introduction to the world of Vagrant. It will help create a foundation of knowledge to guide you through the book. You will learn what Vagrant is, the benefits of Vagrant, what VirtualBox is, and what DevOps is. You'll also learn how Vagrant fits into the DevOps landscape, how it can be used as a DevOps tool, and take a look at other pieces of software.

Chapter 2, *Installing VirtualBox and Vagrant*, Windows, macOS, and Linux, gets your hands dirty by teaching you how to install VirtualBox and Vagrant. We'll cover the three main operating systems: Windows, macOS, and Linux. You'll learn how to navigate both websites (https://www.virtualbox.org and https://www.vagrantup.com) to download, install, and verify the software, once it has been installed.

Chapter 3, *Command Line-Interface - Vagrant Commands*, teaches you about the range of useful commands that Vagrant provides. You'll learn about all of the available commands and sub-commands. You'll also learn about the structure of Vagrant commands, how to use the help command to get more information, and a brief description of what each one does. You will feel confident in managing Vagrant via the command line by the end of this chapter.

Chapter 4, *Discovering Vagrant Boxes - Vagrant Cloud*, covers all aspects of Vagrant boxes. We will look at how to manage them: installation, deletion, and versioning. We will also create a base box that has the minimum requirements for building a Vagrant environment. In this chapter, we will also cover Vagrant Cloud and what it offers you. Vagrant Cloud is a searchable index of Vagrant boxes that are ready to download. We'll cover a range of things, such as how to use the the Vagrant Cloud website, how to search for a specific box, and how to install that box.

Chapter 5, *Configuring Vagrant Using a Vagrantfile*, explores the Vagrantfile, which allows you to easily customize your Vagrant machine. The Vagrantfile offers many different configuration options, such as networking, folder syncing, the multi-machine option, provisioning, and provider-specific settings. You'll also learn the syntax and formatting of a Vagrantfile and how to validate it, once created.

Chapter 6, *Networking in Vagrant*, explains how networking in Vagrant is easily configurable and can be used to create some powerful setups. There are three key networking configuration options that you will learn about in this chapter: port forwarding, public networking, and private networking. You'll learn how to use each one through examples and view the benefits of each.

Chapter 7, *Multi-Machine*, looks at the multi-machine option, which allows you to create multiple Vagrant machines and manage/configure them using a single Vagrantfile. You will create a multi-machine environment that mimics a real-world scenario. You will create one machine that runs a web server and another that runs a database. These machines will communicate using a networking configuration. This will give you a solid foundation and help you to start creating powerful environments using the multi-machine option.

Chapter 8, *Exploring Vagrant Plugins and Syncing Files*, gets into how, although Vagrant offers many features, there may be a specific use case where you require some additional functionality. In this chapter, you will learn all about Vagrant plugins. You will see how easy it is to install and use Vagrant plugins. There are a range of commands and sub-commands to learn about, too. In this chapter, you will also learn about syncing files with Vagrant and the different configuration options available.

Chapter 9, *Shell Scripts - Provisioning*, deals with provisioning in Vagrant, which is another powerful Vagrant feature, giving you the ability to easily provision your Vagrant machines. This chapter acts as an introduction to provisioning and will teach you more about configuration management tools, shell provisioning, and file provisioning. There are multiple configuration options available when using these types of provisioning to learn about, too.

Chapter 10, *Ansible - Using Ansible to Provision a Vagrant Box*, teaches you how to provision a Vagrant environment using Ansible and Ansible playbooks. You will also briefly learn how to install Ansible on your Vagrant machine, before learning how to use Ansible on the host machine to provision the Vagrant box.

Chapter 11, *Chef - Using Chef to Provision a Vagrant Box*, teaches you how to provision a Vagrant environment using Chef and Chef cookbooks. You will look at provisioning the machine using the basic option, Chef Solo, and the advanced option, Chef Client.

Chapter 12, *Docker - Using Docker with Vagrant*, delves into how to provision a Vagrant environment using Docker. We'll look at searching and pulling images from the Docker Hub and then running them as containers. We'll also look at the different options Docker accepts when we're using it as a Vagrant provisioner.

Chapter 13, *Puppet - Using Puppet to Provision a Vagrant Box*, explores how to provision a Vagrant environment using Puppet. You will learn about the two main options available with Vagrant: Puppet Apply and Puppet Agent. Using Puppet Agent, you will see how to connect to a Puppet master and retrieve instructions from that.

Chapter 14, *Salt - Using Salt to Provision a Vagrant Box*, tackles how to provision a Vagrant environment using Salt. You will also learn about Salt states, which allow us to dictate which packages and services should be added into the provisioning.

To get the most out of this book

This book is aimed at both beginners and advanced users. It will teach you how to install the required software. If you already have this software, please check the versions that you have as there may be differences between the version that you have and the version that we use in the book. You may need to upgrade your software. You will need:

- VirtualBox version: 5.2.10
- Vagrant version: 2.0.4
- Ubuntu box (from Vagrant cloud) version: ubuntu/xenial64 20180510.0.0

It's worth reading through each chapter a few times so you don't miss anything. If you need more information or clarification, the official Vagrant website documentation is fantastic.

Download the example code files

You can download the example code files for this book from your account at www.packtpub.com. If you purchased this book elsewhere, you can visit www.packtpub.com/support and register to have the files emailed directly to you.

You can download the code files by following these steps:

1. Log in or register at www.packtpub.com.
2. Select the **SUPPORT** tab.
3. Click on **Code Downloads & Errata**.
4. Enter the name of the book in the **Search** box and follow the onscreen instructions.

Once the file is downloaded, please make sure that you unzip or extract the folder using the latest version of:

- WinRAR/7-Zip for Windows
- Zipeg/iZip/UnRarX for Mac
- 7-Zip/PeaZip for Linux

The code bundle for the book is also hosted on GitHub at https://github.com/ PacktPublishing/Hands-On-DevOps-with-Vagrant. In case there's an update to the code, it will be updated on the existing GitHub repository.

We also have other code bundles from our rich catalog of books and videos available at https://github.com/PacktPublishing/. Check them out!

Download the color images

We also provide a PDF file that has color images of the screenshots/diagrams used in this book. You can download it https://www.packtpub.com/sites/default/files/downloads/ 9781789138054_ColorImages.pdf.

Conventions used

There are a number of text conventions used throughout this book.

`CodeInText`: Indicates code words in text, database table names, folder names, filenames, file extensions, pathnames, dummy URLs, user input, and Twitter handles. Here is an example: "This metadata is usually stored as a JSON document. The filename would be `metadata.json`."

A block of code is set as follows:

```
Vagrant.configure("2") do |config|
    config.vm.box = "base"
  end
```

Any command-line input or output is written as follows:

```
config.vm.network "public_network", ip: "192.168.1.123"
```

Bold: Indicates a new term, an important word, or words that you see onscreen. For example, words in menus or dialog boxes appear in the text like this. Here is an example: "There is a list of supported operating systems, but we need to click on the **Latest Releases on macOS** section."

 Warnings or important notes appear like this.

 Tips and tricks appear like this.

Get in touch

Feedback from our readers is always welcome.

General feedback: Email `feedback@packtpub.com` and mention the book title in the subject of your message. If you have questions about any aspect of this book, please email us at `questions@packtpub.com`.

Errata: Although we have taken every care to ensure the accuracy of our content, mistakes do happen. If you have found a mistake in this book, we would be grateful if you would report this to us. Please visit `www.packtpub.com/submit-errata`, selecting your book, clicking on the Errata Submission Form link, and entering the details.

Piracy: If you come across any illegal copies of our works in any form on the Internet, we would be grateful if you would provide us with the location address or website name. Please contact us at `copyright@packtpub.com` with a link to the material.

If you are interested in becoming an author: If there is a topic that you have expertise in and you are interested in either writing or contributing to a book, please visit `authors.packtpub.com`.

Reviews

Please leave a review. Once you have read and used this book, why not leave a review on the site that you purchased it from? Potential readers can then see and use your unbiased opinion to make purchase decisions, we at Packt can understand what you think about our products, and our authors can see your feedback on their book. Thank you!

For more information about Packt, please visit `packtpub.com`.

1
Introduction

You are about to embark on an exciting journey focused on Vagrant and its role within DevOps. Throughout these chapters, you will learn interesting and useful facts, as well as tips and tricks, about Vagrant. Initially, we will focus on the basics of Vagrant and getting it installed and running on your machine. We will then venture through its ins and outs, by focusing on the important parts of Vagrant, such as its commands, networking, multi-machine, Vagrantfiles, and using configuration management tools, such as Chef, Docker, and Ansible. By the end of this book, you will have solid foundational knowledge about Vagrant and the necessary skill set to start using it on a day-to-day basis as part of your DevOps workflow.

In this chapter, we will create a solid foundation that will help you understand what Vagrant is, what VirtualBox is, and how Vagrant ties into the DevOps landscape. We will learn about the current state of development tools in DevOps and focus on how Vagrant can be used by many different teams in an organisation—not just developers! By the end of this chapter, you will have a good understanding of the basics of Vagrant, VirtualBox, and DevOps.

Getting started with Vagrant and DevOps

In this section, you will be introduced to Vagrant and learn about its features, benefits, and its role in the development tools used in the DevOps world.

Understanding Vagrant

Vagrant is very simple on the surface, but is actually incredibly complex under the hood. It allows you to quickly and effortlessly create virtual environments (known as Vagrant boxes) and customize them. Vagrant easily integrates with multiple providers, such as VirtualBox, VMware, and Docker. These providers actually power the virtual environments, but Vagrant provides a customizable API to that virtual machine.

Vagrant has a large selection of commands, which can be used from the command line/Terminal to manage virtual environments. These commands can quickly download and set up an environment from the Vagrant cloud, which hosts many popular environments, such as Ubuntu or PHP's Laravel.

Vagrant is an important piece of software that can be found in many programmers' toolboxes. It is commonly used to tackle the well-known phrase, *It works on my machine*, by allowing everyone to have a copy of the same environment.

Vagrant was created by Mitchell Hashimoto and released in March 2010. Vagrant is now part of the HashiCorp company, which Mitchell Hashimoto cofounded in 2012 with Armon Dadgar. Vagrant is an open source piece of software that has been built in the Ruby language. It is currently being licensed under the MIT license. Vagrant can be run on macOS, Windows, FreeBSD, and Linux.

Vagrant is essentially another layer in the virtualization stack. It acts as an easily programmable interface to control virtual environments. Vagrant relies on a provider, such as VirtualBox, to power these environments, but it can also configure providers so they work in harmony – an example would be Vagrant controlling how much memory (RAM) an environment has.

Vagrant features

Vagrant offers many features to help you build and configure virtual environments. Vagrant features can be split into a few key areas—Vagrantfile, boxes, networking, provisioning, and plugins. Vagrant can be managed in two key ways – the command line and a Vagrantfile. The command-line approach is often used for admin tasks, such as downloading/importing a new Vagrant box or deleting an old one.

Vagrantfile

A Vagrantfile is a configuration file that uses the Ruby programming language syntax. It is easy to understand and can be quickly tested by making a change and then running the vagrant up command to see whether the expected results happen. A Vagrantfile can easily be shared and added into version control. It's lightweight and contains everything needed for another user to replicate your virtual environment/application.

Boxes

Vagrant boxes are packages that, similar to Vagrantfiles, can be shared and used to replicate virtual environments. Vagrant boxes can be easily downloaded by running the `vagrant box add` command. The Vagrant cloud offers an easily searchable catalogue of boxes. The Vagrant cloud provides lots of information about a box, such as the creator, the version, how many times its been downloaded, and a brief description.

Networking

Vagrant supports three main types of networking when creating virtual environments: public networks, private networks, and port-forwarding. The simplest networking option is port-forwarding, which allows you to access a specific port through the guest operating system into the Vagrant machine. Public and private networking are more complex and offer more configuration, but we will cover that in future chapters.

Provisioning

Provisioning in Vagrant offers you a way to configure the Vagrant machine even more. You can install software and dependencies as the machine is being created. To provision a Vagrant machine, you can use shell scripting, Docker, Chef, Ansible, and other configuration-management software, such as Puppet.

Plugins

Vagrant plugins offer another way to customize and extend the functionality of Vagrant. They allow you to interact with the low-level aspects of Vagrant and often provide new commands to be used as part of the Vagrant command line.

Advantages of Vagrant

Vagrant allows you to easily package up a virtual environment that can be shared among fellow developers. This packaged virtual environment is often referred to as a Vagrant box. A box can be configured to mirror the production environment where your web application or code will be running. This can help minimize any bugs or issues when your application/code is deployed to the production environment.

The beauty of Vagrant's configuration (known as a Vagrantfile) is often small and can be easily edited and tested. The syntax of a Vagrantfile is easy to understand and offers a simple way to build a complex environment.

Vagrant can be used by many different members of a team, including those on the development team, the operations team, and the design team.

Development team

For a developer, Vagrant can allow them to package up their code/application into an easily-sharable fully-fledged development environment. This can then be used by developers using different operating systems, such as macOS, Linux, or Windows.

Operations team

The operations team can easily and quickly test deployment tools and scripts using Vagrant. Vagrant supports many popular deployment tools in the operations/DevOps world, such as Puppet, Docker, and Chef. Vagrant can be a cheaper and faster way to test deployment scripts and infrastructure topologies. Everything can be done locally with Vagrant or it can be used with a service such as Amazon Web Services.

Design team

Vagrant allows the development team and operations team to create virtual environments running code, and applications ready for a designer to easily run this environment on their machine and start making edits to the application. There is no configuration required and feedback can be instant, from when a developer makes a change or a developer has to update the Vagrantfile.

What is VirtualBox?

VirtualBox is one of the many providers that Vagrant supports. VirtualBox is a powerful virtualization tool that allows you to create virtual environments on your existing operating system. It allows you to fully customize a virtual machine's hardware, such as the RAM, CPU, hard drive, audio, and graphics.

VirtualBox was initially released in January 2007 by the company Innotek GmbH, which was later acquired by Sun Microsystems, which, in turn, was acquired by the Oracle Corporation. Oracle is actively maintaining and releasing new versions of VirtualBox.

VirtualBox is built in x86 Assembly, C++, and C. It can run and supports many different operating systems, such as Windows, Linux, Solaris, and OS X.

What is DevOps?

DevOps is a popular term in the IT world at the moment. There are many different opinions as to what DevOps actually is. In simple terms, DevOps is the mix of development and operations. It is essentially creating a sort of "hybrid programmer" who knows about operations and infrastructure, or a system admin who understands programming and can develop applications.

DevOps is a mixture of methodologies, practices, philosophies, and software. DevOps streamlines the whole project life cycle by creating a workflow that works for all departments. There are no rules or laws in DevOps, but generally it's the process of connecting the developers and the infrastructure team by enabling an easy way to develop and ship code.

The beauty of DevOps is that any company can start following its ideas, methodologies, and best practices. Large companies may have a whole DevOps department/team, whereas smaller companies may just need one or two dedicated DevOps employees. In a start-up scenario, where money must be carefully budgeted, one employee may take on the role of developer and also DevOps.

Vagrant for DevOps

In this chapter, you will learn about the current state of development in DevOps, how Vagrant fits into DevOps, and how to use Vagrant as a day-to-day DevOps tool. By the end of this chapter, you will have a much better understanding of how Vagrant can be used for development as part of the DevOps process.

Current state of development within DevOps

As mentioned previously, DevOps is a mixture of software development, operations/system administration, and testing/quality assurance. DevOps is not a new movement, but one that doesn't necessarily have a leader or a set of rules and standards to follow. Every company has their own idea of what DevOps is and how it should be implemented. Many follow similar paths or rough guidelines. Due to the lack of governance with DevOps, the current state of development is varied.

Traditionally, development has always been separate to the operations and server team, but in the last few years, we have seen many DevOps tools bridge that gap and make life easier for both sides.

In the past, when a web developer would build a web application, they would code it, built it locally on their machine, and then FTP (file transfer) the files onto a live (production) server to then run the code—if there were any issues or bugs, the developer would have to make changes to the server environment and debug the code. There are many developers who still use this workflow and it may be because of their environment or because they have no choice in the matter.

Today, a modern web developer's workflow may look like this:

1. The developer writes their code locally but through a virtual environment/machine with a tool such as Vagrant. This allows the developer to set up an environment such as the production one.
2. The developer edits to their code and uses version-control (such as Git or Subversion) to manage changes. The version-control is set up in a way that allows the developer to keep test/new code separate from the production code.
3. A **continuous integration** (**CI**) tool (such as Jenkins or Travis CI) is used to create a pipeline that often has three separate stages—development, staging, and production. The CI tool can be used to run tests against the software, and run scripts such as performing assets by combining and minifying them. The version-control software can be linked into the CI tool, which often triggers these builds and tests. When the developer pushes some new code to the staging environment, tests can be run before it reaches the production environment.
4. Often, if the tests run and there are no issues, the code may be pushed directly into the production branch in the version control. At this point, the CI tool may trigger a new build, which would essentially restart the service that the code applies to. This could be simple or complex, depending on the production environment and software architecture.
5. At some stages during this process, there may be manual intervention by the QA (quality assurance/testing) team or more senior developers who wish to check the code before it goes to production.

Of course, this is just an example workflow and will differ between companies and development teams. The modern workflow may seem much more complicated and tedious, but this is for good measure. At each stage, you'll notice there are checks and tests run before the code can reach a live production environment where real users may be interacting with that code. This can be incredibly important when working with financial software and other business-critical software. This modern workflow greatly reduces the margin of error.

Modern development in the DevOps world is focused on speed and automation. The focus on speed is the ability to quickly build a feature or fix a bug and "push the code to production" (a phrase you might have heard!). This means that single developers or a team of developers have less of a barrier when working on the code. A developer shouldn't worry about configuring servers or environments.

Automation is a big part of DevOps, and that effects the development part too. You can imagine how slow a process it would be if a developer made changes to their code and then had to wait for a member of the operations team to manually run tests and scripts against their changes before letting them know the result.

Vagrant and DevOps

I believe that Vagrant is a key tool in a developer's toolbox in today's DevOps-focused world. Vagrant is essentially a suite of tools that allows the developer to create code but also connect with configuration management tools, such as Puppet, Chef, and Ansible, that are used to automate workflows and environments on servers.

Vagrant's primary focus is on development and enables an easy way for every developer on the team to use the same environment. Within a Vagrant environment, you can run version-control that could link into the CI workflow, which allows you to run tests and move code into different stages.

Using Vagrant as a day-to-day DevOps tool

Vagrant is a flexible tool that enhances day-to-day development by allowing you to easily test out DevOps workflow ideas. It allows you to separate your software code and infrastructure without having to know much about DevOps, infrastructure, servers, and configuration-management tools.

As a day-to-day DevOps tool, Vagrant can be used for many things, including the following:

- Testing software code in different environments and operating systems
- Testing different workflows using configuration-management tools, such as Chef and Puppet
- Working in the same environment as other developers in your team/company
- Easily make changes to Vagrant and see the results instantly
- Running multiple environments/virtual environments to test out networking, file-sharing, and other multi-server use cases

Summary

In this chapter, we learned that Vagrant is a very powerful and flexible tool for helping create virtual environments that can mimic staging and development environments used by your business or application. We looked at the current development state of DevOps, how Vagrant fits into that, and how to use Vagrant as a day-to-day development tool.

In Chapter 2, *Installing VirtualBox and Vagrant*, we will install Vagrant and its provider, VirtualBox. We will look at how to install these pieces of software on a Windows, Mac, and Linux machine. You will also learn how to find out your system's version and its CPU architecture.

Installing VirtualBox and Vagrant

2

VirtualBox is a very important piece of software, which we refer to as a **provider**. Its job is to do the heavy lifting in creating and maintaining virtual machines and environments. Vagrant is essentially a wrapper around a provider (in our case, VirtualBox) and exposes a powerful API that allows you to create and manage virtual machines through code and configuration, such as the Vagrantfile.

Once VirtualBox is installed, we will have very little to do with it. It will sit in the background and await commands from Vagrant to manage virtual machines.

In this chapter, we will start to get our hands dirty with Vagrant. We will look at the following topics:

- Finding the version of your OS
- Finding your CPU architecture
- Installing VirtualBox on Windows, Linux, and macOS
- Installing Vagrant on Windows, Linux, and macOS
- Running Vagrant via the command line/Terminal to see which version of Vagrant you have

By the end of this chapter, you will have a fully working Vagrant and VirtualBox, ready to start creating virtual environments.

Installing VirtualBox and Vagrant on Windows

In this section, you will learn how to install VirtualBox and Vagrant onto a Windows environment, how to find out what your CPU architecture is, and what version of the Windows operating system you are running. We will use an Enterprise edition of Windows 10 64-bit as our example operating system and computer setup.

Prerequisites

Before we install VirtualBox and Vagrant, we need to learn some basic information about your system. This is information required to help you select which package to download.

System version

Finding out which version of Windows you are running will help when choosing which package installer to download. Each version of Windows is different, but we will be covering how to do this using Windows 10.

There are two ways you can do this; the first is a fairly quick and simple way using the Command Prompt in Windows:

1. Press the Windows key + the *R* key (or click Start and search for `run`)
2. This will open a prompt in this prompt, type `winver`
3. Press the *Enter* key and you should see a new `About Windows` screen pop up with all of your OS information

The second way requires a bit more effort, but can be achieved through the Windows graphical user interface:

1. Go into the Windows settings and click **About**
2. You can access the system settings by clicking on the cog in the taskbar or by typing `settings` in the taskbar
3. In the `About` screen, you will see a section titled **Windows specifications**
4. In this section, the part we need to focus on is the **Edit** value
5. The value is `Windows 10 Enterprise Evaluation`

CPU architecture

A system's CPU architecture is generally 32-bit or 64-bit. When you download the VirtualBox or Vagrant software package-installer, you will have to define which version you require.

To find out the CPU architecture for a Windows 10 system, follow these steps:

1. Go into the Windows settings and click **About**
2. You can access the system settings by clicking on the cog in the taskbar or typing `settings` in the taskbar
3. On the `About` screen, you will see a section titled **Device specifications**
4. In this section, the part we need to focus on is the **System type** value
5. The value is `64-bit operating system, x64-based processor`

Installing VirtualBox on Windows 10

Before diving into this section, it's worth mentioning that version 1.8 and later of Vagrant will automatically install VirtualBox onto your system to offer a smoother experience. You can skip this section and move onto the next section, titled *Installing Vagrant on Windows 10*. If you have any issues, please feel free to come back to this section and try to manually install VirtualBox.

Before we install Vagrant, it's wise to install its provider, VirtualBox. To get started, you will need to visit the official VirtualBox website, `https://www.virtualbox.org/`. The best way would be to use your system's internet browser, such as Internet Explorer.

Follow the steps for installation:

1. Click on the **Downloads** link found in the menu on the left side. We're going to focus on the latest version (at the time of writing, this was version 5.2.10).
2. Underneath this section, you should see a list of four **platform packages** links.
3. Click on the **Windows hosts** options. You will be prompted to select a version, such as x86 (32-bit CPU) or AMD64 (64-bit CPU). If this is the case, use the information from **About (CPU Architecture)** and download the appropriate package.
4. When you click on the package, your browser should start the download automatically. Choose **Run** to start the installation immediately after the download completes. You'll be presented with a welcome screen after the installer starts.

5. Click on the **Next** button to continue.
6. To keep things simple, we will stay with the default configuration. This is an opportunity for you to make changes if you so require. This might be as simple as changing the installation location. When you are ready, click on the **Next** button to continue.
7. You should see another screen with customization options. For the sake of simplicity, we will leave all options checked.
8. Click **Next** to continue.

At this stage, you will see a large red `Warning` message. Do not be alarmed, this is normal behavior for the installation. The installer simply needs to temporarily disable and restart the network services on your machine. This will affect anything you are currently doing that requires an internet connection, such as downloading or streaming:

1. When you are ready, click **Yes** to continue to the next screen.
2. This is your final opportunity to make any changes before the VirtualBox software is installed on your system. If you are happy to proceed, click on the **Install** button to continue.
3. Depending on your **User Access Control** security settings, Windows may ask you to confirm the installation. Click **Yes** to allow the software installer to continue.
4. The installation will begin. If you need to cancel for any reason, simply click on the **Cancel** button.
5. The installation should be complete. I would recommend leaving the **Start Oracle VM VirtualBox 5.2.10 after installation** box checked as this will allow you to see the VirtualBox software start. Click on the **Finish** button to continue.
6. You should see an **Oracle VM VirtualBox** shortcut on your desktop (if you left that option ticked during the installation stage). You can open VirtualBox by clicking on that shortcut, or you can use the search bar by typing `virtualbox` and clicking on the result.

After completion, you'll be presented with the screen pertaining to the default installation. Congratulations on completing this step. We will now finish off by installing Vagrant.

Installing Vagrant on Windows 10

It's time to install Vagrant. The following steps are for the installation of Vagrant:

1. Visit the official Vagrant website, `https://www.vagrantup.com/`. The best way would be to use your system's internet browser, such as Firefox. We will stick with the most current, up-to-date version of Vagrant.

2. Click on the **Download 2.0.4** link or the **Download** link in the top navigation menu. You should see the downloads page.

3. We can focus on the Windows section, but you will need to choose either the 32-bit or 64-bit option, depending on your system. My system is a 64-bit one, so I will be choosing that option. The download should start automatically.

4. Choose **Run**, which will download the software and start the installer automatically.

Once the download has finished, the installer should start. You'll be presented with the welcome screen of the installer:

1. Click on the **Next** button to continue.

2. Once you have read the terms and conditions, if you are happy and agree, then tick the option. Click the **Next** button to continue.

3. You can change the installation destination if required. When you are happy, click the **Next** button to continue to the next screen.

4. You have the option to make any changes before Vagrant is installed onto your system. If you don't want to make any more changes, click on the **Install** button.

5. The Windows UAC will ask you whether you are happy to allow the installer to continue. Click on the **Yes** button.

6. Vagrant will start the installation. If you need to cancel for any reason, click on the **Cancel** button.

7. After the successful installation of Vagrant, click on the **Finish** button to close the installer.

8. You must restart your system for Vagrant to be fully installed on your system.

9. Click on the **Yes** button to restart. This will disturb any work you currently have on your system, so make sure you make any saves required.

10. To verify that Vagrant has been installed and that it is running, we will need to use the Command Prompt. To access this, search for `cmd` using the search facility on your system:

```
Command Prompt

Microsoft Windows [Version 10.0.16299.19]
(c) 2017 Microsoft Corporation. All rights reserved.

C:\Users\IEUser>vagrant -v
Vagrant 2.0.4

C:\Users\IEUser>
```

11. Run the `vagrant -v` command by typing it out and pressing *Enter*. You should see an output similar to the preceding screenshot. My Vagrant version is `2.0.4`.

Installing VirtualBox and Vagrant on Linux

In this section, you will learn how to install VirtualBox and Vagrant onto a Linux environment. You will also learn how to find out what your CPU architecture is and what version of the Linux operating system you are running. In this section, we will be using Ubuntu 16.04 64-bit as our example operating system and computer setup.

Prerequisites

Before we install VirtualBox and Vagrant, we need to learn some basic information about your system. This is information required to help you select which package to download.

System version

Finding out what version of Ubuntu you are running will help you choose which package installer to download.

The easiest and quickest way to find out your Ubuntu version is to go into the Terminal and run the `cat /etc/*-release` command.

You should now see some output on the screen. There are a few sections we can focus on these are DISTRIB_DESCRIPTION, VERSION, and VERSION_ID. In my case, it is Ubuntu version 16.04.

CPU architecture

A system's CPU architecture is generally 32-bit or 64-bit. When you download the VirtualBox or Vagrant software package-installer, you will have to define which version you require.

The easiest and quickest way to find out the CPU architecture for a Ubuntu system is to go into the Terminal and run the uname -mrs command.

You should now see some output on the screen. What we are looking for is the last part; in my case, it is showing x86_64.

This is showing that I have a 64-bit CPU architecture. If your system is a 32-bit one, you would likely see either i686 or i386.

Installing VirtualBox on Ubuntu 16.04

Before we install Vagrant, it's wise to install its provider, which is VirtualBox:

1. Visit the official VirtualBox website, https://www.virtualbox.org/. The best way would be to use your system's internet browser, such as Firefox.
2. Click on the **Downloads** option in the navigation menu on the left-hand side.
3. Underneath this section, you should see a list of four **platform packages** links. Click on the **Linux distributions** options.
4. Select a version, such as x86 (32-bit CPU) or AMD64 (64-bit CPU). Use the information from **About (CPU Architecture)** and download the appropriate package. I will choose the Ubuntu 16.04 **AMD64** version to match my system. Click on the link and the download should start automatically. You may be prompted by your system to **Open with** or **Save File**.
5. I will select the **Open with Software Install (default)** option as this will download the package and start the installer automatically. When you have chosen your option, click on the **OK** button.

The Ubuntu installer should now open up. Click on the **Install** option to begin the software installation. Depending on your system's security settings, you may be asked to enter your password. If this is the case, enter your password and click on your **Authenticate** button to continue. We can now check the installation:

1. VirtualBox should be installed on your system, unless any error messages appear during installation. To confirm that VirtualBox has been installed, use the Ubuntu search feature and enter `virtualbox`.
2. You should see it appear underneath the **Applications** section.
3. When you open VirtualBox, you'll be presented with a welcome screen. This is the default installation screen.
4. If you have issues finding VirtualBox on your system, you can also run the `virtualbox` command in Ubuntu's Terminal. If the software is found, it should open VirtualBox.

After completion, you'll be presented with the screen pertaining to the default installation. Congratulations on completing this step. We will now finish off by installing Vagrant.

Installing Vagrant on Ubuntu 16.04

It's time to install Vagrant:

1. Visit the official Vagrant website, `https://www.vagrantup.com/`. The best way would be to use your system's internet browser, such as Firefox.
2. We will stick with the most current version of Vagrant. Click on the **Download 2.0.4** link or the **Download** link in the top navigation menu. You should see the downloads page.
3. As we are using Ubuntu, which is Debian-based, we will focus on that package. Using our knowledge from earlier, we know to choose the 64-bit download option.
4. When you click on the link, your system should prompt you to download the software. I have selected the **Open with Software Install (default)** option as this will download the software and automatically start the installer.
5. Click on the **Install** button to get started.
6. You will be asked to enter your password to start the installation. Enter your password and click the **Authenticate** button.

7. When Vagrant has been installed, you should notice that the **Install** button has now changed into a **Remove** button. If you wish to delete Vagrant, you can use this option:

You can also run the `vagrant -v` command in the Ubuntu Terminal. If Vagrant has been successfully installed, you should see some output. You can see that my system's version is `Vagrant 2.0.4`.

Installing VirtualBox and Vagrant on macOS

In this section, you will learn how to install VirtualBox and Vagrant onto a macOS environment. You will learn how to find out what your CPU architecture is and what version of the Mac operating system you are running. In this section, we will be using macOS High Sierra 10.13.3 64-bit as our example operating system and computer setup.

Prerequisites

Before we install VirtualBox and Vagrant, we need to learn some basic information about your system. This is information required to help you select which package to download.

System version

Finding out what version of macOS you are running will help you choose which package installer to download.

One of the easiest and quickest ways to find out system information for Mac is to run the `sw_vers` command in the Terminal:

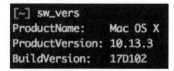

There are two key values here we can focus on: `ProductName`, which is `Mac OS X`; and `ProductVersion`, which is `10.13.3`.

CPU architecture

A system's CPU architecture is generally 32-bit or 64-bit. When you download the VirtualBox or Vagrant software package-installer, you will have to define which version you require.

We can run the `sysctl hw.cpu64bit_capable` command, which lets us know whether our system is capable of running 64-bit software. In this screenshot of my system, you can see the returned value is `1`:

This means that I have a 64-bit-capable Mac system. If your value returns as empty or `0`, then your system only supports 32-bit.

Installing VirtualBox on Mac OS 10.11.3

Before diving into this section, it's worth mentioning that version 1.8 and later of Vagrant will automatically install VirtualBox onto your system to offer a smoother experience. You can skip this section and move onto the next section, titled *Installing Vagrant on macOS*. If you have any issues, please feel free to come back to this section and try to manually install VirtualBox.

Before we install Vagrant, it's wise to install its provider, which is VirtualBox:

1. Visit the official VirtualBox website, `https://www.virtualbox.org/`. The best way would be to use your system's Internet Browser, such as Firefox.
2. Click on the **Downloads** link found in the navigation menu on the left-hand side.

3. This should load the downloads page of the website. For this book, we will be using VirtualBox version 5.2.10, so please navigate to that section of the page. When presented with the screen, click on the **OS X hosts** link and this should start the download automatically on your system.

4. Once the download has finished, click on the `.dmg` file to run the VirtualBox installer package. Your Mac system will open and verify the installer. You will see a temporary screen with a few different options. Follow step 1 by clicking and opening the `VirtualBox.pkg` file.

5. The VirtualBox installer will run. Click the **Continue** button.

6. The system has verified that you can install this VirtualBox software. Click on the **Continue** button to begin the installer process.

7. On this next screen, you have the option to change the install location. You may do this as you wish, but for the sake of simplicity and consistency, we will leave it as the default location. If you are happy to proceed, click on the **Install** button.

8. Your system may ask you to log in to allow the installer to continue. Please enter your username (this may already be filled out) and your system password. Then click the **Install Software** button to continue.

9. The installer will install the files and configurations that it requires. If there are no issues during installation, you should see a `The ivag`

10. To verify and run VirtualBox, you can find it in your applications folder and possibly on your desktop. When you open the installer, you should see the VirtualBox default welcome screen.

Congratulations! You have successfully installed VirtualBox on your macOS system.

Installing Vagrant on macOS 10.13.3

It's time to install Vagrant:

1. Visit the official Vagrant website, `https://www.vagrantup.com/`. The best way would be to use your system's internet browser, such as Firefox.

2. Click on **Download 2.0.4** on the homepage or the **Download** link in the top-right navigation menu. This will load the Vagrant download page.

3. The current version of Vagrant only supports the 64-bit version of macOS. We will be using that one. Click on the link to start the download.

4. Once the download has finished, click on the `.dmg` file to open the Vagrant installer. The Mac system will open and verify the Vagrant installer.

5. Once the verification has completed, you will see a temporary splash screen. Click on the `vagrant.pkg` icon to run the installer.

6. You should see the `Introduction` screen of the installer. Click on the **Continue** button to start the process.

7. You have the option to change Vagrant's installation location.You may do this as you wish, but for the sake of simplicity and consistency, we will leave it as the default location. If you are happy to proceed, click on the **Install** button.

8. Your system may ask you to log in to allow the installer to continue. Please enter your username (this may already be filled out) and your system password. Click the **Install Software** button to continue.

9. The installation will begin. If the installation was successful, you should see the `The installation was successful` screen.

You may now click on the **Close** button to close the installer. Vagrant has no graphical user interface, so we can verify that is has been installed by running the `vagrant -v` command, which should output which version of Vagrant that we are running:

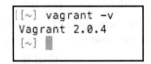

As you can see from my Terminal output, the macOS system is running Vagrant version `2.0.4`. Congratulations! You have successfully installed Vagrant onto your macOS system.

Summary

In this chapter, we've learned how to install Vagrant and its provider, VirtualBox, onto Windows, Mac, and Linux machines. You now have the base environment to start using Vagrant and creating virtual environments.

In `Chapter 3`, *Command Line-Interface - Vagrant Commands*, we will learn all about Vagrant's commands and subcommands. These powerful commands offer us the full feature set of Vagrant, from basic features, such as returning Vagrant's software version, to managing boxes, such as importing and installing them from the Vagrant cloud.

3
Command Line-Interface - Vagrant Commands

In this chapter, we will learn how to control Vagrant through its various commands and sub-commands. Vagrant has no graphical user interface so we will be running the commands through a Terminal/Command Prompt. By the end of this chapter, you will have a strong fundamental knowledge of the Vagrant commands and their uses. We will cover the following topics:

- Vagrant commands, sub-commands, and flags
- Formatting commands
- General Vagrant commands and sub-commands
- Vagrant's configuration commands and sub-commands
- Day-to-day Vagrant commands and sub-commands
- Application-specific Vagrant commands and sub-commands
- Troubleshooting

Vagrant command overview

Vagrant is primarily a command-line only tool. By default, there is no graphical user interface, although it is possible to find a few third-party ones online. Vagrant offers a simple and powerful collection of over 25 commands and sub-commands.

To get started with Vagrant commands, open up your Command Prompt / Terminal and run the `vagrant --help` command. You should now see a list of common commands, these include `box`, `destroy`, and `status`.

To view the fill list of available and less-commonly-used commands, run `vagrant list-commands`. You will now see a larger list of commands with a brief explanation about each one.

To get more information on a specific command and to view its sub-commands, add the --help flag at the end of the command you want to learn more about. An example is vagrant box --help, which would return the following:

```
[~] vagrant box --help
Usage: vagrant box <subcommand> [<args>]

Available subcommands:
        add
        list
        outdated
        prune
        remove
        repackage
        update
```

When a command has sub-commands available, you can also add the --help flag to that sub-command to learn more. In this case, our command would be vagrant box add --help, which would return:

```
[~] vagrant box add --help
Usage: vagrant box add [options] <name, url, or path>

Options:

    -c, --clean                     Clean any temporary download files
    -f, --force                     Overwrite an existing box if it exists
        --insecure                  Do not validate SSL certificates
        --cacert FILE               CA certificate for SSL download
        --capath DIR                CA certificate directory for SSL download
        --cert FILE                 A client SSL cert, if needed
        --location-trusted          Trust 'Location' header from HTTP redirects
and use the same credentials for subsequent urls as for the initial one
        --provider PROVIDER         Provider the box should satisfy
        --box-version VERSION       Constrain version of the added box

The box descriptor can be the name of a box on HashiCorp's Vagrant Cloud,
or a URL, or a local .box file, or a local .json file containing
the catalog metadata.

The options below only apply if you're adding a box file directly,
and not using a Vagrant server or a box structured like 'user/box':

        --checksum CHECKSUM         Checksum for the box
        --checksum-type TYPE        Checksum type (md5, sha1, sha256)
        --name BOX                  Name of the box
    -h, --help                      Print this help
```

As you can see in the screenshot, there is a wealth of information available about this sub-command. Vagrant is very well-documented and anything that you cannot find via the command-line/Terminal, you should be able to find on the Vagrant website: https://www.vagrantup.com/.

Vagrant commands in depth

In this section, you will learn about all of the available Vagrant commands and sub-commands. We will explore the most common commands and what each one does. We will look at errors with regards to commands and how to overcome them.

We will split the commands and sub-commands into the following four categories:

- General
- Configuration
- Day-to-day
- Application-specific

By the end of this section, you will have a good understanding of which commands and sub-commands are available, what they do, and how you can use them on a daily basis.

A brief note on formatting commands

In this chapter, I will use certain keywords as placeholders. These placeholders are for you to enter values into the commands and sub-commands. A typical placeholder will look like this: [INSERT VALUE]. An example would be vagrant login --user [INSERT VALUE], where [INSERT VALUE] would be something such as myusername and the final command that you input would be vagrant login --user myusername. There is no need for capital letters or square brackets.

When you see the [VMNAME] placeholder, this refers to a specific Vagrant machine name that you want to run the command against on your system. The default Vagrant machine is called default, so an example command would be vagrant resume default, which would resume the machine from a suspended state.

General Vagrant commands and sub-commands

The general commands and sub-commands in Vagrant are not category-specific. They may only get used once or serve an incredibly specific purpose.

The list-commands command

The `list-commands` command will list all available commands within the main `vagrant` command scope. It will alphabetically list each command and give a brief description.

Options/flags

There is only one flag for this command, `-h/--help`, which will print the help screen for this command.

An example is the `vagrant list-commands --help` command.

The help command

The `help` command will show you the correct syntax for a command and list a selection of the most popular Vagrant commands.

The version command

The `version` command will return the version of Vagrant that is currently installed on your system, the latest version available online, and supply a website URL to the downloads page of the Vagrant website.

Options/flags

There is only one flag for this command, `-h/--help`, which will print the help screen for this command.

An example is the `vagrant version --help` command.

The global-status command

The `global-status` command will return information about all of the Vagrant environments associated with the current user. It will return the Vagrant environment ID, name, provider, state, and directory. This command can be useful for giving you an overview into what is happening on your system with the Vagrant environments.

Options/flags

There are two flags for this command:

- -h/--help: Prints the help screen for this command
- --prune: Prunes any invalid entries

An example is the vagrant global-status --help command.

Vagrant's configuration commands and sub-commands

In this section, we will look at Vagrant's configuration commands and sub-commands. These are often used to configure Vagrant, such as installing a package or taking a snapshot of an environment.

The login command

The login command is used to log into your HashiCorp Vagrant Cloud account. Logging into the Vagrant Cloud will allow you to access and download protected boxes and the Vagrant Share service, which allows you to share your Vagrant environment with anyone.

Options/flags

There are six flags for this command:

- -c/--check: Checks to see whether you are already logged in
- -d/--description [INSERT VALUE]: Takes a parameter to set a description of the token
- -k/--logout: Logs you out if you are already logged in
- -t/--token [INSERT VALUE]: Takes a parameter to set the Vagrant Cloud token
- -u/--username [INSERT VALUE]: Takes a parameter to specify your Vagrant Cloud email or username
- -h/--help: Prints the help screen for this command

An example is the vagrant login --check command.

The package command

The `package` commands allow you to create a Vagrant box out of a running Vagrant environment.

Options/flags

There are five flags for this command:

- `--base [INSERT VALUE]`: Takes a parameter of the name of a virtual machine in VirtualBox to package as a base box. This flag only works if you are using the VirtualBox provisioner.
- `--output [INSERT VALUE]`: Takes a parameter to name the output file.
- `--include [INSERT VALUE, INSERT VALUE]`: Takes comma-separated parameters to include additional files in this packaging process.
- `--vagrantfile [INSERT VALUE]`: Takes a parameter of the Vagrantfile you wish to package into this box.
- `-h/--help`: Prints the help screen for this command.

An example is the `vagrant package --help` command.

The snapshot command

The `snapshot` command allows you to manage snapshots of Vagrant environments. You can save, delete, and restore snapshots. Only certain providers support snapshotting If your provider does not, Vagrant will return a warning when this command is run.

sub-commands

There are six sub-commands available for the `snapshot` command:

- `vagrant snapshot delete [INSERT VALUE] [INSERT VALUE]`: The first parameter is the virtual machine name and the second parameter is the name of the snapshot you wish to delete.
- `vagrant snapshot list [INSERT VALUE]`: The parameter can optionally be the Vagrant machine name. This command will list all available snapshots on your system or all snapshots for a certain Vagrant machine if the parameter is specified.

- `vagrant snapshot push`: This can be used to create a new snapshot of a running Vagrant environment. It will add this onto the Snapshot stack.
- `vagrant snapshot pop`: This can be used as an opposite to the `push` command to reverse a snapshot that has been pushed.
- `vagrant snapshot save [INSERT VALUE] [INSERT VALUE]`: This saves a snapshot of the current machine. It's similar to the `push` command, but it is recommended that you do not mix this command with `push` or `pop` as it is unsafe. The first parameter is the virtual machine name and the second parameter is the snapshot name.
- `vagrant snapshot restore [INSERT VALUE] [INSERT VALUE]`: This restores a supplied snapshot. The first parameter is the virtual machine name and the second is the name of the snapshot you wish to restore to.

The provider command

The `provider` command will return the provider for the current running machine, or it can accept an environment ID.

Options/flags

There are three flags for this command:

- `--install`: Attempts to install the provider
- `--usable`: Checks whether the provider is usable
- `-h/--help`: Prints the help screen for this command

An example is the `vagrant provider --install` command.

The plugin command

The `plugin` command allows you to manage Vagrant plugins. You can install, list, repair, uninstall, and update plugins.

sub-commands

There are seven sub-commands available for the `plugin` command:

- `vagrant plugin expunge`: Removes all user-installed plugins. This will remove any data and dependencies associated with them. This is a useful command if you wish to delete them all in one go.
- `vagrant plugin install [INSERT VALUE]`: Installs a plugin by supplying its name as the command's parameter. You can install a plugin from a known Gem or from a local Gem file on your system.
- `vagrant plugin license [INSERT VALUE] [INSERT VALUE]`: Installs a proprietary Vagrant plugin license. The first parameter is the plugin name and the second is the licence file.
- `vagrant plugin list`: Lists all installed plugins on your system. It will list plugin information, such as its version. This command is useful for finding out which plugins and versions you have installed.
- `vagrant plugin repair`: Attempts to repair any plugins where there has been an issue and it is not working correctly. The issue could be during the installation of a custom plugin or an error with the `plugins.json` file.
- `vagrant plugin uninstall [INSERT VALUE]`: Deletes a plugin using a supplied plugin name as the first parameter. This command supports multiple parameters, with each one being a plugin name. You can delete one or multiple plugins using this command.
- `vagrant plugin update [INSERT VALUE]`: Updates a specific plugin if the first parameter is supplied as the plugin's name. If no parameter is supplied, this command will update all installed plugins.

The cap command

The `cap` command allows you to run or check the capabilities of a guest machine. These capabilities are often guest-specific and are configured specifically, for example, in Vagrant plugin development.

Options/flags

There are two flags for this command:

- `--check [INSERT VALUE] [INSERT VALUE]`: Checks for a certain capability. The first parameter is the capability name and the second parameter is the capability arguments. This command will not run the capability.
- `-h/--help`: Prints the help screen for this command.

An example is the `vagrant cap --help` command.

Day-to-day Vagrant commands and sub-commands

Day-to-day Vagrant commands and sub-commands are the ones you will use the most. These commands are generally used to manage your Vagrant boxes, such as creating, starting, and stopping them.

The box command

The `box` command allows you to manage Vagrant boxes on your system. You can install, update, remove, and prune boxes.

sub-commands

There are seven sub-commands available for the `box` command:

- `vagrant box add [INSERT VALUE]`: Adds and downloads a Vagrant box to your system. This box can then be used in your Vagrantfile to create a Vagrant machine.
- `vagrant box list`: Lists all installed boxes installed on your system.
- `vagrant box outdated`: Checks whether the current Vagrant box is outdated. You can add the `--global` flag, which will check all installed Vagrant boxes.
- `vagrant box prune`: Removes old versions of installed boxes. It will ask for confirmation if you are currently using an old version of a box it wants to delete.
- `vagrant box remove [INSERT VALUE]`: Removes a Vagrant box by name as the first parameter supplied.

- `vagrant box repackage [INSERT VALUE] [INSERT VALUE] [INSERT VALUE]`: Repackages a Vagrant box into a `.box` file using the name as the first parameter, the provider as the second parameter, and the version as the third parameter. You can get the parameter values using the `vagrant box list` command. The box can then be distributed.
- `vagrant box update`: Checks and updates the current box you are using. You can supply the `--box [INSERT VALUE]` flag where the first parameter is the box name that you wish to specifically update.

The destroy command

The `destroy` command will stop and delete a Vagrant machine.

Options/flags

There are three flags for this command:

- `-f/--force`: Destroys the Vagrant machine without asking you for confirmation.
- `--parallel/--no-parallel`: Enables or disables parallelism only if the provider supports it. We are using VirtualBox as the provider in this book, and at the time of writing it does not support parallel execution. Running this flag will enable the `force` flag too.
- `-h/--help`: Prints the help screen for this command.

An example is the `vagrant destroy --force` command.

The halt command

The `halt` command will stop/halt a running Vagrant machine.

Options/flags

There are two flags for this command:

- `--force [INSERT VALUE]`: Forces the running machine to shut down. If your machine has not saved, you may lose data when running this command it is like switching off the computer's power source. You can specify a machine name or ID using the optional parameter.

- -h/--help: Prints the help screen for this command.

An example is the vagrant halt --force command.

The init command

The init command generates a new Vagrantfile, which is used to configure new Vagrant environments.

Options/flags

There are six flags for this command:

- --box-version [INSERT VALUE]: Adds a version of the box supplied as the first parameter into the Vagrantfile
- -f/--force: Overwrite an existing Vagrantfile if there is already one in the same directory
- -m/--minimal: Generates a minimal Vagrantfile that will remove anything not required, such as comments
- --output [INSERT VALUE]: Uses an output path specified by the first parameter
- --template [INSERT VALUE]: Uses a custom Vagrantfile template when its path is supplied as the first parameter
- -h/--help: Prints the help screen for this command

An example is the vagrant init --force command.

The port command

The port command returns port-mapping from the guest machine to the Vagrant environment.

Options/flags

There are three flags for this command:

- --guest [INSERT VALUE]: Outputs specific port information when the first parameter supplied is the port available on the guest machine. It will return the host-mapped port. This command can be useful for certain network-level debugging or testing.

- `--machine-readable`: Returns/displays a more machine-readable output.
- `-h/--help`: Prints the help screen for this command.

An example is the `vagrant port --machine-readable` command.

The provision command

The `provision` command will provision a Vagrant machine from an available Vagrantfile. If successful, you will have a running and fully-provisioned Vagrant environment.

Options/flags

There are two flags for this command:

- `--provision-with [INSERT VALUE]`: Provisions the Vagrant machine with a specified provisioner. You can use multiple provisioner types by suppling the parameter as a comma-separated list.
- `-h/--help`: Prints the help screen for this command.

An example is the `vagrant provision --help` command.

The push command

The `push` command will deploy code using a method that you have configured in the Vagrantfile. You can use FTP/SFTP and Heroku as the deployment methods.

Options/flags

There is only one flag for this command, `-h/--help`, which will print the help screen for this command.

An example is the `vagrant push --help` command.

The reload command

The `reload` command is used when you make a change to the Vagrantfile and wish to apply that to the running machine. This command will stop, apply the new Vagrantfile, and start up the environment.

Options/flags

There are three flags for this command:

- `--provision/--no-provision`: Enables or disables provisioning during the reload process.
- `--provision-with [INSERT VALUE]`: Provisions the Vagrant machine with a specified provisioner. You can use multiple provisioner types by suppling the parameter as a comma-separated list.
- `-h/--help`: Prints the help screen for this command.

An example is the `vagrant reload --no-provision` command.

The resume command

The `resume` command will start up a paused Vagrant environment. It can be used after the `vagrant halt` command.

Options/flags

There are three flags for this command:

- `--provision/--no-provision`: Enables or disables provisioning as the machine resumes.
- `--provision-with [INSERT VALUE]`: Only uses certain provisioners specified in the first parameter. To use multiple, you can supply a comma-separated list. The supplied value can be a provisioner by name or by type.
- `-h/--help`: Prints the help screen for this command.

An example is the `vagrant resume --no-provision` command.

The status command

The `status` command will return the status of a Vagrant machine. It will return information such as `stopped` or `running`.

Options/flags

There is only one flag for this command, -h/--help, which will print the help screen for this command.

An example is the vagrant status --help command.

The suspend command

The suspend command is similar to the vagrant halt command, but instead of completely stopping and shutting down the machine, it will save the state this uses extra disk space on your guest machine, but when you start the machine back up again, it will start quickly and from that exact point. There will be no lengthy boot-up process as if you were starting it from cold.

Options/flags

There is only one flag for this command, -h/--help, which will print the help screen for this command.

An example is the vagrant suspend --help command.

The up command

The up command will start up a Vagrant environment. During the start process, it will also provision the machine, similarly to the vagrant provision command.

Options/flags

There are seven flags for this command:

- --provision/--no-provision: Enables or disables provisioning when the Vagrant machine is starting up.
- --provision-with [INSERT VALUE]: Only uses certain provisioners specified in the first parameter. To use multiple, you can use a comma-separated list. The supplied value can be a provisioner by name or by type.
- --destroy-on-error/--no-destroy-on-error: Destroys a machine if there is a fatal error. This is the default behavior unless you use the --no-destroy-on-error flag.

- `--parallel/--no-parallel`: Enables or disables parallelism only if the provider supports it. We are using VirtualBox as the provider in this book, and at the time of writing it does not support parallel execution. If you run the command, nothing will happen.
- `--provider [INSERT VALUE]`: Uses a provider supplied as the first parameter.
- `--install-provider/--no-install-provider`: Attempts to install the provider if possible and it isn't installed.
- `-h/--help`: Prints the help screen for this command.

An example is the `vagrant up --no-parallel` command.

The validate command

The `validate` command will validate a Vagrantfile and return any errors. It checks for issues within the Vagrantfile, such as incorrect syntax.

Options/flags

There is only one flag for this command, `-h/--help`, which will print the help screen for this command.

An example is the `vagrant validate --help` command.

Application-specific Vagrant commands and sub-commands

Application-specific Vagrant commands and sub-commands that focus on an external application or piece of software not directly related to Vagrant or VirtualBox. In this section, we'll cover the Docker, RDP, RSync, SSH, and PowerShell commands and sub-commands.

The docker-exec command

The `docker-exec` command is used to run commands directly into a running `docker` container. This is done when using Docker as Vagrant's provider.

Options / flags

There are eight flags for this command:

- `--no-detach`/`--detach`: Enables or disables the command running in the background.
- `-i`/`--interactive`: Keeps the standard input (STDIN) open even if not attached.
- `--no-interactive`: Doesn't keep the standard input (STDIN) open even if not attached.
- `-t`/`--tty`: Enables a pseudo-tty, called a pty.
- `--no-tty`: Disables a pseudo-tty, called a pty.
- `-u [INSERT VALUE]`/`--user [INSERT VALUE]`: Sends a user or UID as the first parameter with the command.
- `--prefix`/`--no-prefix`: Enables or disables a prefix output with the machine name. This can be useful for differentiating between machines/containers.
- `-h`/`--help`: Prints the help screen for this command.

An example is the `vagrant docker-exec --no-tty` command.

The docker-logs command

The `docker-logs` command will return the logs from a running container. This is done when using Docker as Vagrant's provider.

Options/flags

There are three flags for this command:

- `--no-follow`/`--follow`: Enables or disables streaming Docker log data into the output.
- `--no-prefix`/`--prefix`: Enables or disables a prefix output with the machine name. This can be useful for differentiating between machines/containers.
- `-h`/`--help`: Prints the help screen for this command.

An example is the `vagrant docker-logs --no-follow` command.

The docker-run command

The `docker-run` command is very similar to the vagrant `docker-exec` command in that it allows you to run a command on a Docker container. It has fewer options and less configurability compared to the `docker-exec` command. Again, this command is used when using Docker as Vagrant's provider.

Options/flags

There are six flags for this command:

- `--no-detach`/`--detach`: Enables or disables the command to run in the background
- `-t`/`--tty`: Enables a `pseudo-tty`, called a `pty`.
- `--no-tty`: Disables a `pseudo-tty`, called a `pty`
- `-r`/`--rm`: Removes the container after execution
- `--no-rm`: Doesn't remove the container after execution
- `-h`/`--help`: Prints the help screen for this command

An example is the `vagrant docker-run --no-detach` command.

The rdp command

The `rdp` command is used to create a client for a remote desktop with the Vagrant environment. This can only be used with Vagrant environments that support the remote-desktop protocol.

Options/flags

There is one flag for this command, `-h`/`--help`, which will print the help screen for this command.

An example is the `vagrant rdp --help` command.

The rsync command

The `rsync` command will force a sync between any folders that have been configured to use RSync as the sync option, to the remote machine. A sync will often only happen when you manually start up or reload a Vagrant environment.

Options/flags

There is one flag for this command, `-h/--help`, which will print the help screen for this command.

An example is the `vagrant rsync --help` command.

The rsync-auto command

How to run `vagrant rsync-auto`: The `rsync-auto` command is similar to the `vagrant rsync` command in that is forces a sync between any configured RSync folders, but it will now listen to all configured directories for any changes to files and RSync them automatically.

Options/flags

There are three flags for this command:

- `--poll`: Forces polling of the filesystem. This option does not have great performance and can be slow.
- `--no-poll`: Disables polling of the filesystem.
- `-h/--help`: Prints the help screen for this command.

An example is the `vagrant rsync-auto --no-poll` command.

The ssh command

The `ssh` command will connect you to a remote Vagrant machine using the SSH protocol/connection. This command gives you access to the machine's shell, which allows you to run commands directly on the machine.

Options/flags

There are five flags for this command:

- `-c [INSERT VALUE]/--command [INSERT VALUE]`: Runs a command directly via SSH using the first parameter supplied.
- `-p/--plain`: Connects in plain mode, leaving you to choose the authentication.
- `-t/--tty`: Enables `tty` when you run an SSH command. This is the default value.

- `--no-tty`: Disables `tty` when you run an SSH command.
- `-h/--help`: Prints the help screen for this command.

An example is the `vagrant ssh --plain` command.

The ssh-config command

The `ssh-config` command will generate a configuration that can be used in an SSH configuration file, which can then be used to SSH into the Vagrant machine.

Options/flags

There are two flags for this command:

- `--host [INSERT VALUE]`: Names the host used for the config when the first parameter is supplied
- `-h/--help`: Prints the help screen for this command

An example would be the `vagrant ssh-config --host testname` command.

The powershell command

The `powershell` command will open a PowerShell connection to a Vagrant machine. The `powershell` command will only work with guest machines and Vagrant machines that support it. For example, when trying to run this command on a guest machine, such a Mac, the following error will be returned:

```
Your host does not support PowerShell. A remote PowerShell connection can
only be made from a windows host.
```

Options /flags

There are two flags for this command:

- `--c [INSERT VALUE]/--command [INSERT VALUE]`: Runs a PowerShell command supplied as the first parameter
- `-h/--help`: Prints the help screen for this command

An example is the `vagrant powershell --help` command.

A typical Vagrant workflow using commands

In this section, you will see how a few Vagrant commands and sub-commands can create a basic workflow:

1. Make sure you are in a new empty directory (this isn't necessary but helps keep the project separate from your other files).

2. Run `vagrant init ubuntu/xenial64` `https://vagrantcloud.com/ubunutu/xenial64.box`. This will create a default Vagrantfile, but the box will be set as Ubuntu 16.04.4 64-bit version. The first parameter is the official box name and the second is the download URL for it.

3. Run the `vagrant validate` command to make sure the Vagrantfile is error-free and ready to go. There should not be any errors here as we are just using the basic default Vagrantfile. You should see the `Vagrantfile validated` `successfully` message returned.

4. Start up the Vagrant machine. To do this, run the `vagrant up` command. If you do not have that Ubuntu box installed, Vagrant will download it during the provisioning process. It may take some time depending on your internet speed.

5. During the boot process, you will see many things happen. Vagrant will configure network connections, import the box, configure and start SSH services, forward any ports between your machine and the guest Vagrant machine, and mount any shared folders.

6. When the box is finished booting and Vagrant has finished configuring, you will be able to log in via SSH and run commands directly in the Vagrant environment. To do this, run the `vagrant ssh` command.

7. After a few seconds, you should see the Ubuntu Terminal and the message of the day. The first line should say something similar to `Welcome to Ubuntu` `16.04.04 LTS`. You can now run commands inside the Vagrant environment such as installing Ubuntu packages.

8. Exit out of here and stop the Vagrant machine. Run the `exit` command inside the Ubuntu Terminal.

9. You can check on the status of the Vagrant environment by running the `vagrant` `status` command. This will return a list of Vagrant machines on your system. You should see your machine still running, the name will likely be `Default` and the status will be `running (virtualbox)`, where VirtualBox is the provider we have used to power the Vagrant machine.

10. Let's save a snapshot of the environment's current state. We can run the `vagrant snapshot save default first_snapshot` command, which tells Vagrant to save a snapshot using the machine with the name of default and it to call the snapshot `first_snapshot`.

11. To confirm the snapshot has been saved, run the `vagrant snapshot list` command, which should return `first_snapshot`. The command will only return one snapshot at first as that is all we have saved, but eventually you will see a list as you save more. You can then use a snapshot to restore the environment to that save.

12. Stop the Vagrant machine by running the `vagrant suspend` command. This will take a few minutes.

Congratulations! You have successfully created a Vagrant machine, installed Ubuntu, used SSH, saved a snapshot of the Vagrant machine, and suspended it.

This is a fairly simple workflow as we have not done any work on the machine or installed any additional features. In later chapters, we will look at how to customize the Vagrantfile and change the provision process. We will also look at provisioning a Vagrant machine using configuration-management tools, such as Chef and Ansible.

Troubleshooting

With such a large selection of Vagrant commands, sub-commands, parameters, and flags, it is very easy to enter the command and get an error message.

Vagrant is very good at returning an error if you enter the wrong command. There can be a few reasons a command might return an error:

- You are trying to run a command when no Vagrant machines are running
- You are trying to run a command against a Vagrant machine with a non-existent or incorrect name/ID, or one that has been deleted
- There is a typo in your command
- You have the parameters in the wrong order
- You have not specified any parameters when they are required
- You have the flags in the wrong order
- You have not specified any flags when they are required

- You are running a provider-specific command when you are not actually using that provider
- You are running an OS-specific command when you are not actually using that OS

Here are a few troubleshooting tips:

- Read the error message slowly to see what you may have missed.
- Run the `vagrant [INSERT VALUE] --help` command where `[INSERT VALUE]` is the command you are trying to run. This will give you the syntax, order, parameters, and flags for that command.
- Make sure you haven't got any typos in your command string.
- It can also be worth checking the Vagrantfile in case that is causing any issues or interfering in some way. You can run the `vagrant validate` command to make sure it's OK.
- You can always visit the official Vagrant website to make sure that the version of Vagrant you have has the command available/supports the command that you are trying to run.
- If you are completely stuck and cannot troubleshoot the issue, searching for the specific error message can be incredibly useful. You will likely come across someone who has the same problem, normally on a website such as Stack Overflow or the GitHub issues section of the Vagrant project.
- In the most extreme cases, you may need to uninstall Vagrant (and sometimes VirtualBox) and then restart your machine. You will then need to reinstall Vagrant (and possibly VirtualBox). A fresh install can sometimes be last option but the right answer!

Summary

In this chapter, we covered Vagrant's commands and sub-commands. You should now have a good understanding as to what each command does and in what scenarios to use it. Feel free to flick back and use this chapter as a reference.

In `Chapter 4`, *Discovering Vagrant Boxes - Vagrant Cloud*, we will learn about Vagrant boxes and the Vagrant Cloud. You will learn how to install a Vagrant box, manage it, create your own Vagrant box, and search for other community- and company-created boxes on the Vagrant Cloud platform.

4

Discovering Vagrant Boxes - Vagrant Cloud

In this chapter, you will learn all about Vagrant boxes. You will learn what a box is, and how to manage one via the Vagrant commands and sub-commands that we covered in the previous chapter. We will also learn about the Vagrant Cloud, which is an online catalog of public and private Vagrant boxes available for you to search and install on your system – ready to use for your own Vagrant environment!

By the end of this chapter, you will have a solid foundational knowledge of Vagrant boxes and the Vagrant Cloud. You will also learn about the following topics:

- The anatomy of a Vagrant box
- How to install Vagrant boxes
- How to remove Vagrant boxes
- Box versioning
- What is the Vagrant Cloud?
- How to create your own box (repackaged)
- How to upload your custom box to the Vagrant Cloud
- Enterprise solutions for Vagrant boxes

Understanding Vagrant boxes

A Vagrant box is a specific package format for containing Vagrant environments. A Vagrant box file uses the `.box` file extension. A Vagrant box can be used with any platform and system that Vagrant supports to create the same environment by following the steps in the box file.

Vagrant box file anatomy

A Vagrant box file is made up of three components: box file, box metadata, and box information. These components help package everything you need into one file. Various parts of these components are used by Vagrant when using and installing a new box to create the correct environment. Let's dive into the three components and see what each one does.

Box file

The box contains different information depending on the provider. It is provider-specific and could be in several different formats, such as ZIP, `tar.gz`, or TAR. This information is not used by Vagrant but is instead passed on to the provider.

Box metadata

The box catalog metadata is generally used with the Vagrant cloud platform. It contains information such as the box name, different versions, descriptions and different supported providers, and any URLs to specific box files. This metadata is usually stored as a JSON document. The filename would be `metadata.json`.

Box information

The box information is the extra details that you can add. These extra details are displayed when a user runs the `vagrant box list --box-info` command. You can set information for the author name/company and a URL. This file is a JSON document and the filename would be `info.json`.

How to install a Vagrant box

In this section, you will learn how to install a Vagrant box. There are a number of ways that Vagrant boxes can be installed:

- A URL that points directly to the box file
- A shorthand/alias for a public box name, such as `debian/jessie64`
- A file path or URL to a box in a specific catalog

Often, the simplest option is to use shorthand as it does not require you to know the full box URL or catalog URL.

When a Vagrant box supports multiple providers, you will be given the option to choose which one you wish to install:

```
[~] vagrant box add https://app.vagrantup.com/laravel/boxes/homestead
⟹ box: Loading metadata for box 'https://app.vagrantup.com/laravel/boxes/homes
tead'
This box can work with multiple providers! The providers that it
can work with are listed below. Please review the list and choose
the provider you will be working with.

1) hyperv
2) virtualbox
3) vmware_desktop
```

You can also use the `--provider` flag to specify which provider version of the box you wish to install. Vagrant offers an easy-to-use option, such as the preceding screenshot, or provides a much more comprehensive utility when using the command line.

Direct URL to box file

Using this option requires you to know the full URL to a box file and you must use the `--name` flag so Vagrant has some reference to the box. This reference helps with updating and versioning.

Here is an example of the command: `vagrant box add --name "mybox" http://www.example.com/boxname.box`.

This command would install the `boxname.box` box, giving it the name `mybox`, and downloading it from the `www.example.com` domain.

Shorthand/alias to box file

This method is fairly simple and straightforward if you know theshorthand/alias name for the box.

Here is an example of the command: `vagrant box add debian/jessie64`.

This command will install the 64-bit *Jessie* version of the Debian OS. You can often find the shorthand/alias box name by searching online via search engines or using the Vagrant Cloud platform.

A file path or URL to a box in a specific catalog

This method is similar to the first method mentioned in the *Direct URL to box file* section, where you can use a URL or file path to download and install a box file directly.

Here is an example of the command: `vagrant box add https://app.vagrantup.com/ubuntu/boxes/trusty64`.

This command will install the 64-bit *Trusty* version of Ubuntu. You do not need to use the `--name` flag for this method as Vagrant will get this information from the box metadata and box information files.

How to delete a Vagrant box

At some point, you may need to delete a Vagrant box from your system. There may be a few reasons:

- To free up system space
- To remove a corrupt version
- To remove an old version that is no longer required

Whatever your reason, in this section, you will learn how to delete Vagrant boxes. Before deleting a box, it's worth getting the correct name/format in case you accidentally delete the wrong box!

To list the available boxes on your system, run the `vagrant box list -i` command, which will return the installed boxes on your system, their name, their provider, and the latest version. Using the `-i` flag will supply an additional description that may help you choose the correct box.

Deleting a specific version of a box

It is possible to delete a specific version of a Vagrant box without deleting the box entirely from your system. You may do this to free up space from older box versions that you no longer use on your system.

You can run the `vagrant box prune --dry-run` command to view a list of outdated box version on your system. The output of this command will show you boxes that will be kept (if you choose to run the `prune` command) and any boxes that will be removed.

Here is the example output of the preceding command:

```
[~] vagrant box prune --dry-run
The following boxes will be kept...
bento/ubuntu-15.04      (virtualbox, 2.2.5)
laravel/homestead       (virtualbox, 5.1.0)
packer-test             (aws, 0)
packer-test-2           (aws, 0)
packer_amazon-ebs_aws   (aws, 0)
puphpet/debian75-x64    (virtualbox, 20151201)
puphpet/ubuntu1404-x64  (virtualbox, 20151201)
ubuntu/trusty64         (virtualbox, 20160913.0.0)
ubuntu/xenial64         (virtualbox, 20180510.0.0)

Checking for older boxes...
Would remove laravel/homestead virtualbox 2.0.0
```

If you wish to remove all outdated boxes from your system, run the `vagrant box prune` command.

To delete a specific box version, you can run the `vagrant box remove [BOXNAME] --box-version [BOXVERSION]` command, where the first parameter is the box name and the second is the specific version. Here is the example output:

```
[~] vagrant box remove laravel/homestead --box-version 2.0.0
Removing box 'laravel/homestead' (v2.0.0) with provider 'virtualbox'...
```

Deleting all versions of a box

To remove all versions of a Vagrant box, you can run the `vagrant box remove [BOXNAME]` command, where the first parameter is the box name. When running this command, your terminal will ask for confirmation before deleting the box.

Here is the example output:

```
[~] vagrant box remove packer-test
Removing box 'packer-test' (v0) with provider 'aws'...
```

If, for any reason, you just want to delete the box without confirmation, you can run the `vagrant box remove [BOXNAME] --force` command, which uses the `--force` flag.

Box versioning

Vagrant boxes can have multiple versions that can be installed on your system. In the previous section, we discussed how to `prune` outdated box versions and how to delete a box by a specific version.

Vagrant Cloud

In this section, we will focus on the Vagrant Cloud. We will learn what it is, what it is used for, how you can use it, and how you can search the Vagrant Cloud for Vagrant boxes to install on your system.

Understanding the Vagrant Cloud

The Vagrant Cloud is HashiCorp's cloud platform that allows you to search, upload, and download Vagrant boxes. It allows you to create accounts and offers three different account tiers, which are a mix of free and paid.

Vagrant Cloud website

You can access the Vagrant Cloud website by visiting `https://app.vagrantup.com`, although it may redirect you to `https://app.vagrantup.com/boxes/search`.

There are currently three different pricing tiers, which offer different features depending on what you need. Here are the three tiers:

- **Free**: This option provides unlimited public boxes
- **Personal**: This option provides unlimited public boxes and an option of $5 per month per private box
- **Organization**: This options provides unlimited public boxes, an option of $25 per month per private box, and the ability to share private boxes with teams

To choose the right tier, it really depends on your use case and what you wish to use the Vagrant Cloud for. You can start with the free tier and always upgrade if you need to.

Installing a Vagrant box found on the Vagrant Cloud – Part 1, Search

Let's use the search feature to find a box that we can install on our system. The search feature is fairly simple, but does offer a few filters. You can access the search box at `https://app.vagrantup.com/boxes/search`.

You should see a section similar to the following screenshot:

There are three different options available for searching the Vagrant Cloud:

- The main text input area in which you can type pretty much anything – the box name, operating system, architecture, and included software.
- You can filter by **Provider**, such as **virtualbox**, **vmare**, and docker. If you have no preference, you can choose the **any** option.
- You can also sort the results by **Downloads** (number of total downloads), **Recently Created**, and **Recently Updated**.

Let's search for a `Laravel` (this is a PHP framework) box that supports the VirtualBox provider and let's sort it by **Downloads**:

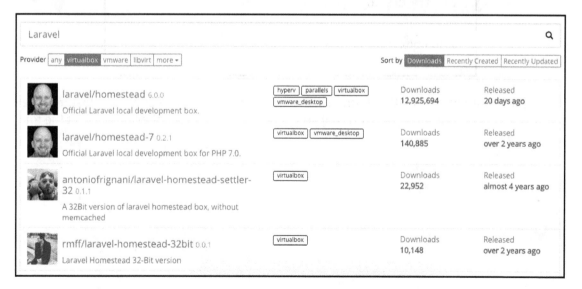

Let's click on the first result to get more information about that box:

There is a wealth of information found on this page, including the box version history. The latest box version is listed by most recent so you should always see the latest one at the top.

The first section, titled *How to use this box with Vagrant*, gives a two basic examples about installing and using this box on your system. The default tab shown is the **Vagrantfile** one, which shows you three lines that can be added to your **Vagrantfile**. The second tab, titled **New**, shows you how to install and run the box using commands in your terminal, you can see that option here:

Let's look at version 6.0.0, which is the *currently-released version*. You can see when this version was created (in our case, it was 20 days ago) and there is a GitHub URL available where you can view the release information for that specific version.

In this section, you can also view which providers this version supports and the file size for this box. In our case, we can see that three providers are supported for the 6.0.0 version: **hyperv**, **vmware_desktop**, and **virtualbox**. We can see that the file size for **hyperv** is **1.26 GB**, and for **vmare_desktop** and **virtualbox** the file size is **1.38 GB**.

Installing a Vagrant box found on the Vagrant Cloud – Part 2, Install

Now that we have found the Vagrant box we want, let's install it and use it on our system. We will use the `init` command to create a new **Vagrantfile** and install the box.

First create a new empty directory, move into that directory, and run the `vagrant init laravel/homestead` command, as described on the Vagrant Cloud website:

```
[laravelbox] vagrant init laravel/homestead
==> vagrant: A new version of Vagrant is available: 2.1.1!
==> vagrant: To upgrade visit: https://www.vagrantup.com/downloads.html

A `Vagrantfile` has been placed in this directory. You are now
ready to `vagrant up` your first virtual environment! Please read
the comments in the Vagrantfile as well as documentation on
`vagrantup.com` for more information on using Vagrant.
```

You should now see a new Vagrantfile in your current directory, run the `ls` command to see:

```
[laravelbox] ls
Vagrantfile
```

Let's look inside the Vagrantfile. I've opened the Vagrantfile using the Atom text editor. Let's focus on the first few lines (not the comments):

```ruby
                  V Vagrantfile
1  # -*- mode: ruby -*-
2  # vi: set ft=ruby :
3
4  # All Vagrant configuration is done below. The "2" in Vagrant
5  # configures the configuration version (we support older styl
6  # backwards compatibility). Please don't change it unless you
7  # you're doing.
8  Vagrant.configure("2") do |config|
9    # The most common configuration options are documented and
10   # For a complete reference, please see the online documenta
11   # https://docs.vagrantup.com.
12
13   # Every Vagrant development environment requires a box. You
14   # boxes at https://vagrantcloud.com/search.
15   config.vm.box = "laravel/homestead"
```

You can see on line number 15 that the `config.vm.box` key has been set a value of `laravel/homestead`. This is what the `init` command does, it creates/initializes a new Vagrantfile and sets a specified value depending on the parameter of the command.

We can now start up the Vagrant box, which will install the `laravel/homestead` box. Run the `vagrant up` command:

```
[laravelbox] vagrant up
Bringing machine 'default' up with 'virtualbox' provider...
==> default: Box 'laravel/homestead' could not be found. Attempting to find and
install...
    default: Box Provider: virtualbox
    default: Box Version: >= 0
==> default: Loading metadata for box 'laravel/homestead'
    default: URL: https://vagrantcloud.com/laravel/homestead
==> default: Adding box 'laravel/homestead' (v6.0.0) for provider: virtualbox
    default: Downloading: https://vagrantcloud.com/laravel/boxes/homestead/versi
ons/6.0.0/providers/virtualbox.box
    default: Progress: 4% (Rate: 5228k/s, Estimated time remaining: 0:05:36)
```

If you do not have the box installed on your system, it will first have to download the `.box` file. The file is approximately 1.38 GB (according to the Vagrant Cloud website for the current version we are trying to download, which is 6.0.0); it may take some time to download depending on your internet connection/speed.

Once installed, you should see a green success message and the box will start to be imported:

```
==> default: Successfully added box 'laravel/homestead' (v6.0.0) for 'virtualbox
'!
==> default: Importing base box 'laravel/homestead'...
Progress: 40%
```

Once imported, Vagrant will continue the box initialization, which will configure networking, SSH, and storage mounting. You can start experimenting with the box by connecting via SSH by running the `vagrant ssh` command:

```
[laravelbox] vagrant ssh
Welcome to Ubuntu 18.04 LTS (GNU/Linux 4.15.0-20-generic x86_64)
```

Let's run a simple command against the Vagrant box to make sure everything is working. Once you've run the `ssh` command, run the `php -v` command, which will output the PHP version installed on the system. PHP should be installed as that is one of the requirements of the Laravel framework. You should see an output similar to the following:

```
vagrant@vagrant:~$ php -v
PHP 7.2.4-1+ubuntu18.04.1+deb.sury.org+1 (cli) (built: Apr  5 2018 08:55:11) ( N
TS )
Copyright (c) 1997-2018 The PHP Group
Zend Engine v3.2.0, Copyright (c) 1998-2018 Zend Technologies
```

We can see that PHP is installed and the version is `7.2.4-1`. If you wish to exit out of the Vagrant box, simply run the `exit` command. You can view `vagrant status` to view the status of the Vagrant box, the value should be `virtualbox (running)`. You can stop the command by running the `vagrant halt` command:

```
[laravelbox] vagrant halt
==> default: Attempting graceful shutdown of VM...
```

You can now check the status again by running the `vagrant status` command again:

```
[laravelbox] vagrant status
Current machine states:

default                   poweroff (virtualbox)

The VM is powered off. To restart the VM, simply run `vagrant up`
```

You can see that the status has changed to `poweroff (virtualbox)`.

Uploading a Vagrant box to the Vagrant cloud

In this section, you will learn how to create your own Vagrant box and how to upload that box to the Vagrant cloud. You will learn how to package up a base box to work with the VirtualBox provider.

Before we continue, please create an account with the Vagrant Cloud platform. This can be done at `https://app.vagrantup.com/account/new` or by visiting the Vagrant Cloud website and clicking on the **Create an Account** link in the menu.

Creating a Vagrant box

Before we can upload anything to the Vagrant Cloud platform, we need to create a box. Our Vagrant box will be a repackaged version of the `ubuntu/xenial64` base box that can be found on the Vagrant Cloud platform. To keep it simple, we will simply be repackaging this box and uploading it using a different name.

First of all, you will need to make sure you have the `ubuntu/xenial64` box installed on your system. You can check this by running the `vagrant box list` command. You can see that I have it installed on my system as it appears in the following screenshot:

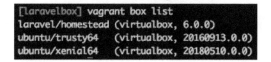

If you do not have it installed, run the `vagrant box add ubuntu/xenial64` command to install the box on your system.

Let's run the box to make sure it's working correctly. Run the `vagrant init ubuntu/xenial64` command to generate a basic Vagrantfile and then run the `vagrant up` command to get the box up and running.

Once up and running, you should be able to `vagrant ssh` into the machine. Everything should be working, let's now `exit` out of the box and run the `vagrant halt` command to stop the machine.

Now it's time to set up the Vagrant box in the Vagrant Cloud dashboard. Log into your account and click on the **Dashboard** button, you should see another button titled **New Vagrant Box**. Click on that button and you should see the following screen:

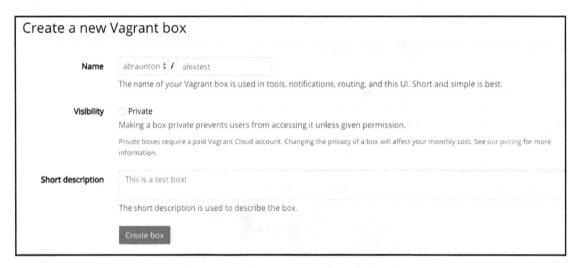

The name is split into two parts: your username and the box name separated by a slash. My box will be accessible via `abraunton/alextest`, but it would be better to use a more descriptive name. You cannot use private mode unless you have a paid account. I would recommend adding in a **Short description** when possible. Click on the **Create box** button to continue when you are ready.

We now need to add a version in for this box. Let's start with `0.0.1` as this is the very first iteration of our box. You can also add in a **Description** for this specific version:

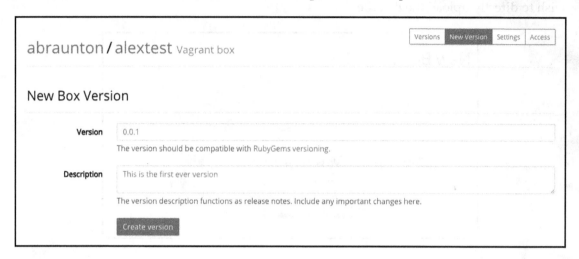

Click on the **Create version** button when you are ready. We now need to add a provider to our Vagrant box. You can do this by clicking the **Add a provider** button, within your new version:

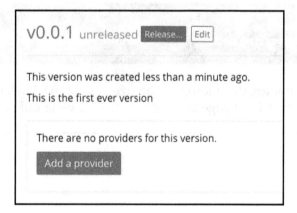

You will now need to choose which provider this box file supports. We will be sticking with VirtualBox in this example and selecting the **Upload to Vagrant Cloud** option as we wish to directly upload the box file:

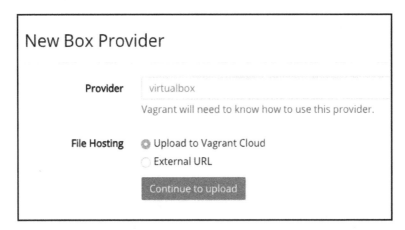

Before we can continue, we must package the box into a file. You can do this by running the `vagrant package --output alextest.box` command in the same directory as the box you wish to package:

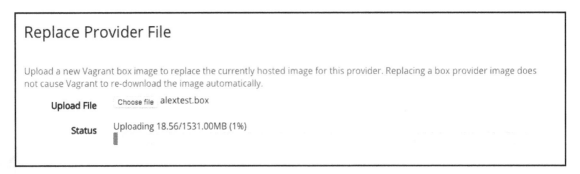

This may take a few minutes, depending on the size of your machine. Once completed, head back to the Vagrant Cloud page and click the **Continue to upload** button:

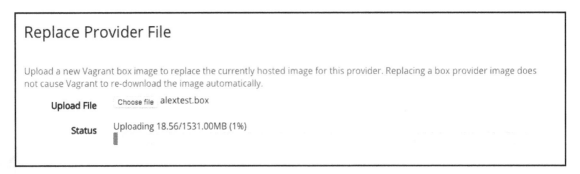

Choose the file (it must be a `.box` file) and the upload should start automatically. This may take some time, depending on your internet speed. When complete, the status should change to **Upload Complete**.

Congratulations! You have successfully created and uploaded a Vagrant box onto the Vagrant Cloud. You can see this by clicking on the **Dashboard** menu; this will now list any boxes you have added:

You can see that under the **My Vagrant Boxes** section, my `abraunton/alextest` box has appeared. It has the description that we added in and it also states that there are **No released versions**. This means that the box is unavailable for download but we can change that. Click into the box and you should see the following message:

Scroll down and you should see the 0.0.1 version of the box that we have uploaded. Click on the **Release...** button to start the release process:

You will now see a confirmation screen and will be required to click on the **Release version** button to complete the process:

abraunton / alextest Vagrant box

Release Box Version

⚠ This version is unreleased. Upon releasing, it will be available to users from Vagrant.

Release version

You should now see a green **Successfully released** message. Congratulations! You have publicly released your first Vagrant box onto the Vagrant Cloud:

Successfully released

Now for the real test; let's check to make sure our box is available and that we can install and run it on our system. Run the `vagrant init abraunton/alextest --box-version 0.0.1` command:

```
[alextestbox] vagrant init abraunton/alextest --box-version 0.0.1
```

This will generate a Vagrantfile telling Vagrant to use the **abraunton/alextest** box and the specific version of 0.0.1. Next, run the `vagrant up` command. This will install our box from the Vagrant Cloud and create our environment:

```
[alextestbox] vagrant up
Bringing machine 'default' up with 'virtualbox' provider...
==> default: Box 'abraunton/alextest' could not be found. Attempting to find and
    install...
    default: Box Provider: virtualbox
    default: Box Version: 0.0.1
==> default: Loading metadata for box 'abraunton/alextest'
    default: URL: https://vagrantcloud.com/abraunton/alextest
==> default: Adding box 'abraunton/alextest' (v0.0.1) for provider: virtualbox
    default: Downloading: https://vagrantcloud.com/abraunton/boxes/alextest/vers
ions/0.0.1/providers/virtualbox.box
    default: Progress: 3% (Rate: 5955k/s, Estimated time remaining: 0:05:16)
```

If your box is available and has a release, you should be able to successfully download it. If all goes well, you should see this green message in your terminal:

```
==> default: Successfully added box 'abraunton/alextest' (v0.0.1) for 'virtualbox'!
```

The Vagrant box should now be up and running, let's `vagrant ssh` into the box and see what we get. Upon SSHing in, you should see the Ubuntu welcome message. That's correct, as we repackaged an Ubuntu box:

```
[alextestbox] vagrant ssh
Welcome to Ubuntu 18.04 LTS (GNU/Linux 4.15.0-20-generic x86_64)
```

Congratulations! You have successfully installed and run your Vagrant box from the Vagrant cloud. You may now stop the machine, remove the box, or experiment with it. Have fun!

Enterprise solutions for Vagrant boxes

If you are looking for a more enterprise solution for hosting and managing your boxes, there are services available to you.

These services offer products and features such as the following:

- Box-hosting
- Box versioning
- Private box access and security
- Local repositories for offline box access
- Advanced/smart search

An example of this type of service is **Artifactory**, which is developed by JFrog. Artifactory is a binary artifact-management tool. Artifactory allows you to host, manage, and version Vagrant boxes in a secure manner. Their focus on security often appeals to enterprise customers who may need to host sensitive data.

Artifactory offers a type of onsite hosting by using local repositories. It still allows you to share access between employees and teams within your organization. These repositories can be cloned to other Artifactory services if access needs to be shared outside local networks.

Depending on your requirements and company rules, a solution such as this may be worth looking into. The Vagrant Cloud is an excellent service to consider as well.

Summary

In this chapter, we covered many aspects of Vagrant boxes. We learned what a Vagrant box is, what forms a box, how to install a box, how to delete a box, box versioning, and we created our own (repackaged) box and uploaded it to the Vagrant Cloud. We then installed that box from the Vagrant Cloud and tested it on our system.

In `Chapter 5`, *Configuring Vagrant Using a Vagrantfile*, we will focus on the Vagrantfile. We have briefly mentioned this file but we have not used it to its full potential yet. The Vagrantfile is used to configure Vagrant and offers a very powerful but easy-to-use syntax. You will learn how to create a Vagrantfile, how to validate one, and the syntax it uses.

5
Configuring Vagrant Using a Vagrantfile

In this chapter, we will focus on configuring Vagrant by using Vagrantfiles. We will focus on the key aspects of a Vagrantfile, such as its structure and syntax. At the end of this section, we will have covered the following topics:

- Understanding Vagrantfiles
- Creating a Vagrantfile
- Vagrantfile structure and syntax
- Troubleshooting a Vagrantfile

Understanding Vagrantfiles

A Vagrantfile is the main way of configuring a Vagrant environment. This file has no extension as such; it is simply found on your system as `Vagrantfile`, not `.Vagrantfile` or `vagrantfile.Vagrantfile`.

Using a Vagrantfile allows you to manage your Vagrant environment dependencies and settings. It is a best practice to have one Vagrantfile per Vagrant project, and to include the Vagrantfile in your source control.

One of the main benefits of using a Vagrantfile is the ability to share that file with any other developer that has Vagrant installed. They will be able to simply run the `vagrant up` command to pull in any dependencies, such as boxes, and to set up any configuration to get the same Vagrant environment up and running as you.

Creating a Vagrantfile

Before we create our own Vagrantfile, let's first create and move into a new directory. In this example, we will create a new directory called vagrantfiletest to keep things simple! Run the following commands in the given order:

1. mkdir vagrantfiletest
2. cd vagrantfiletest
3. vagrant init

By using the vagrant init command, we have now initialized a new Vagrantfile in our current vagrantfiletest directory, as shown in the following screenshot:

```
[~] mkdir vagrantfiletest
[~] cd vagrantfiletest
[vagrantfiletest] vagrant init
==> vagrant: A new version of Vagrant is available: 2.1.1!
==> vagrant: To upgrade visit: https://www.vagrantup.com/downloads.html

A `Vagrantfile` has been placed in this directory. You are now
ready to `vagrant up` your first virtual environment! Please read
the comments in the Vagrantfile as well as documentation on
`vagrantup.com` for more information on using Vagrant.
[vagrantfiletest] ls
Vagrantfile
```

The default Vagrantfile has a basic structure to get you started. If you wish to create a very minimal shell then you can run either the vagrant init --minimal or the vagrant init -m command, either of which will generate a very basic Vagrantfile with no comments or additional settings, as follows:

```
Vagrant.configure("2") do |config|
  config.vm.box = "base"
  end
```

Now let's move on to the next section and learn more about a Vagrantfile's syntax.

Vagrantfile syntax

A Vagrantfile uses the Ruby language syntax but no knowledge of Ruby is required. It is a simple, expressive, and easy-to-understand language when using the Vagrantfile. In most cases you will simply be setting a variable and a value, such as config.vm.box = "ubuntu/trusty64", which sets the box to ubuntu/trusty64, the 64-bit version of Ubuntu 14.04.

A Vagrantfile configuration is contained within the `configure` block. The first line is `Vagrant.configure("2") do |config|` and the last line is `end`. Within this block we can define all sorts of values, such as the Vagrant box, networking, filesystems, provisioning, and more.

Vagrantfile options

In this section, we will cover the various sections that are available to configure in a Vagrantfile. You will learn how to configure the virtual machine directly, configure the provider (VirtualBox), and configure how Vagrant will connect to your machine via SSH or any other communicator.

Vagrant machine configuration (config.vm)

Using the `config.vm` namespace, we will look at configuring certain parts of the Vagrant machine, such as box information and miscellaneous settings including synced folders, provision, and providers. The configurable elements are as follows:

- `config.vm.boot_timeout` is used to specify (in seconds) how long Vagrant will wait for the machine to start up and become available for use. The default time is 300 seconds.
- `config.vm.box` is used to set a specific box for the machine. You can reference a box already installed on your system or a shorthand syntax box name from the Vagrant cloud, such as `ubuntu/trusty64`.
- `config.vm.box_check_update` is used by Vagrant to check whether the box you have selected or the box being used by the current machine is up to date. The default setting is `true` but only certain box types can be checked for an update – mainly Vagrant cloud boxes. If an update is found during the Vagrant startup process, a yellow message will be displayed on the screen to the user.
- `config.vm.box_download_checksum` is used to compare the checksum of a box and a given checksum; if they do not match then it will throw an error. Vagrant will only perform this check when a box needs to be downloaded. This value requires the `config.vm.box_download_checksum_type` value to be set.

- `config.vm.box_download_checksum_type` is the checksum hash type used when comparing checksum values used by the `config.vm.box_download_checksum` value. There are a few supported options here, and they are `md5`, `sha1`, and `sha256`.
- `config.vm.box_download_client_cert` is used to supply a path to a client certificate that is used when downloading a box. There is no default value for this setting.
- `config.vm.box_download_ca_cert` is used to supply the path to a CA certificate bundle that is used when downloading a box directly. The default value for this uses the Mozilla CA certificate bundle.
- `config.vm.box_download_ca_path` is used to supply a path to a directory containing CA certificates when downloading a box directly. Similarly, the default value used is the Mozilla CA certificate bundle.
- `config.vm.box_download_insecure` is used to validate SSL certificates from the server. If `true` is set then no validation will be done. If the box URL is HTTPS then the SSL certificates will be verified.
- `config.vm.box_download_location_trusted` is used to trust all redirects when the value is set to `true`. The default process is for Vagrant to trust the initial request, using any specified credentials.
- `config.vm.box_url` is used to set a specific box URL. This is similar to `config.vm.box` but it does not support the shorthand Vagrant cloud syntax for box names; if `config.vm.box` has been set in the Vagrantfile, you do not need to specify a value here. The value specified can be a single URL or multiple URLs that will be tried in order. If you have already configured other settings such as certificates, they will be applied to all URLs supplied. The Vagrantfile does also support local files using the `file://` abbreviation and scheme.
- `config.vm.box_version` is used to specify what box version to use. This value supports constraints separated by commas such as (greater than and equal to) >= 0.2 and < 2.0 (less than), where Vagrant would look for a box version that's between 0.2 and less then 2.0 . Vagrant will try and get the latest box version within these constraints. The default value used is >= 0, which signifies the latest version available.
- `config.vm.communicator` is used to set the communicator type that connects to the guest box. The default value is `ssh` but it is recommended that Windows guests use `winrm`.

- `config.vm.graceful_halt_timeout` is used to set the time (in seconds) that Vagrant will wait for the machine to halt. This applies when the `vagrant halt` command is used, and the default value is 60 seconds.
- `config.vm.guest` is used to set the guest OS that will be running within the machine. Vagrant will attempt to auto-detect the correct OS used. This information is required to perform certain OS-specific values such as network configuration. The default value for this is `:linux`.
- `config.vm.hostname` is used to set a hostname for a machine. The value should be provided as a string, for example `elite`. The default value is `nil`, which means that Vagrant will not manage the hostname. This hostname (if it's a provider) will be set during boot.
- `config.vm.network` is used to set the machine's network options. There are quite a few options available for this setting, and they will be covered in a later chapter. Some of the main options include `forwarded_port`, `private_network`, and `public_network`. Each option has various sub-values or sub-options that you can set.
- `config.vm.post_up_message` is used to display a message to the user after the `vagrant up` command is run. This is similar to a message of the day found on servers or other pieces of software that you can log into.
- `config.vm.provider` is a configuration block used to set provider-specific values. Each provider supports different values but you can have multiple configuration blocks that target different providers. As we are using VirtualBox as our provider, we can set specific values such as `memory`, which sets the RAM, `cpus`, which sets the CPU core count, and `gui`, which when set to `true` will actually open the Vagrant machine in a GUI so you can interact with it.
- `config.vm.provision` is used to specify a provisioner that can install and configure software during the creation process. This is quite an advanced topic and something we will cover in later chapters. Certain providers supported are Chef, Ansible, Puppet, and a standard script.
- `config.vm.synced_folder` is used to configure synced folders between your host machine and the guest machine. This will allow you to create or edit a file on your system (in the synced folder) and have that change made and become visible in the Vagrant machine.
- `config.vm.usable_port_range` is used to specify a port range that Vagrant can use. The default value or port range is `220..2250`. Vagrant will use these values for any port collisions that happen.

Vagrant SSH configuration (config.ssh)

Using the `config.ssh` namespace we will look at configuring Vagrant so it connects to a guest machine using SSH. Here, we will look at certain values such as SSH username, password, ports, and keys, as follows:

- `config.ssh.username` is used to set the username that Vagrant will use when trying to connect via SSH. The default username is `vagrant`.
- `config.ssh.password` is used to set the password that Vagrant will use when trying to connect via SSH.
- `config.ssh.host` is used to set the hostname or IP address used when SSHing in. This value is often left blank by default as the provider can auto-detect the correct value.
- `config.ssh.port` is used to set the port used for SSHing into. The default value used is 22.
- `config.ssh.guest_port` is used to set the port number that SSH will run on on the guest machine. Vagrant can use this along with `config.ssh.port` to intelligently connect to the correct SSH port. This is often used if there is a forwarded port.
- `config.ssh.private_key_path` is used to set the path to a private key that you want to use when connecting to a machine. The default value is an insecure key that Vagrant and many public boxes use.
- `config.ssh.keys_only` is used when you wish to use Vagrant-provided SSH keys. The default setting is `true`.
- `config.ssh.verify_host_key` is used to perform host-key validation. The default value is `false`.
- `config.ssh.forward_agent` is used to enable agent forwarding over SSH. The default value is `false`.
- `config.ssh.forward_x11` is used to enable X11 forwarding over SSH. The default value is `false`.
- `config.ssh.forward_env` is used to supply an array of host environment variables to the guest machine.
- `config.ssh.insert_key` is used when `true` (as per the default setting) to insert a new keypair to use with SSH, replacing the insecure, default Vagrant keypair. When set to `true`, this value is also used with the `config.ssh.password` option.
- `config.ssh.proxy_command` is used to proxy a command-line command through SSH via `stdin`.

- `config.ssh.pty` is not recommended unless you really need to use it. This option, when set to `true`, will use `pty` for provisioning. `pty` can break certain parts of Vagrant so be wary when using it.
- `config.ssh.keep_alive` will send keep alive packets via SSH every 5 seconds to keep the connection alive when the value is set to `true`.
- `config.ssh.shell` is used to set the shell you wish to use when running SSH commands from Vagrant.
- `config.ssh.export_command_template` is the template used when generating environment variables in the active session.
- `config.ssh.sudo_command` is used to set the command when running a `sudo` command. The default value is `sudo -E -H %c`, where `%c` is replaced by the command to run.
- `config.ssh.compression` is used to send a compression setting when connecting via SSH if the value is set to `true`. To disable this, set the value to `false`.
- `config.ssh.dsa_authentication` is used to send the DSA authentication setting when connecting via SSH if the value is set to `true`. To disable this, set the value to `false`.
- `config.ssh.extra_args` is used to pass additional commands into the SSH executable. It supports a single value or an array of values. This can be sent to enable more advanced actions with SSH, such as reverse tunneling.

Vagrant settings (config.vagrant)

Using the `config.vagrant` namespace we will look at configuring Vagrant specifically. There are not many options available within this namespace compared to the others we have already looked at. The commands for the `config.vagrant` namespace are as follows:

- `config.vagrant.host` is used to set the host machine that is running Vagrant. The default value is `:detect`, which allows Vagrant to intelligently auto-detect the host. Certain features Vagrant offers are host-specific and this value is only recommended to be changed if auto-detection fails.
- `config.vagrant.sensitive` is used to supply a list or array of items that will not be displayed in Vagrant's output or logged output. These values are often passwords or keys.

Other Vagrantfile settings

There are two other namespace settings that you can configure in the Vagrantfile. We will not be focusing on these in detail in this book, but the following section will offer an overview.

WinRM settings (config.winrm)

The `config.winrm` namespace is used to configure Vagrant when using a Windows guest machine. To use these settings, you must set your `config.vm.communicator` setting to `winrm`.

There are around 12 different configuration options available, which include `config.winrm.username`, `config.winrm.password`, `config.winrm.port`, and `config.winrm.transport`. Using the `config.winrm` namespace gives you much more control over how Vagrant behaves when using a Windows guest machine.

WinSSH settings (config.ssh and config.winssh)

This uses the `config.ssh` namespace, similar to namespaces we discussed earlier. This uses the WinSSH software, which is used for the Windows-native port of OpenSSH. Vagrant's official documentation states that WinSSH is in the *pre-release* stage and is therefore not yet production-ready.

There are around 17 different options available, which are a mixture of the `config.ssh` and `config.winssh` namespace, these include: `config.ssh.username`, `config.ssh.password`, `config.winssh.forward_agent`, `config.winssh.upload_directory`, and `config.winssh.export_command_template`.

Troubleshooting a Vagrantfile

A Vagrantfile can be quite a complex collection of configuration options. There are multiple options, such as basic string values, configuration blocks, array values, and much more. It can be quite common to write out a Vagrantfile, go to run `vagrant up` or a similar command, and be faced with an error.

An example of a Vagrant error after running the `vagrant up` command is as follows:

```
[vagrantfiletest] vagrant up
There is a syntax error in the following Vagrantfile. The syntax error
message is reproduced below for convenience:

/Users/alexbraunton/vagrantfiletest/Vagrantfile:24: syntax error, unexpected tID
ENTIFIER, expecting keyword_end
  # accessing "localhost:8080" will access port 80 on
                    ^
```

Let's dissect the error in the preceding screenshot. The first clue is a reference to the line number `Vagrantfile:24`; in other words, line 24 of the Vagrantfile. This error also gives us the type of error: `syntax error, unexpected tIDENTIFIER, expecting keyword_end # accessing "localhost:8080" will access port on`. This could mean that a config block or loop has no end value set, or we have tried to set an incomplete variable.

An easy way to check a Vagrantfile after making any changes and trying to run or provision a Vagrant machine is by using the `vagrant validate` command. In the following screenshot, you can see that we still get the same error and output from Vagrant even with the `vagrant validate` command:

```
[vagrantfiletest] vagrant validate
There is a syntax error in the following Vagrantfile. The syntax error
message is reproduced below for convenience:

/Users/alexbraunton/vagrantfiletest/Vagrantfile:24: syntax error, unexpected tIDENTIFIER, expecting keyword_end
  # accessing "localhost:8080" will access port 80 on
                    ^
```

Now let's open up the Vagrantfile and take a closer look at line 24, as shown in the following screenshot:

```
     V Vagrantfile
1   # -*- mode: ruby -*-
2   # vi: set ft=ruby :
3
4   # All Vagrant configuration is done below. The "2" in Vagrant.configure
5   # configures the configuration version (we support older styles for
6   # backwards compatibility). Please don't change it unless you know what
7   # you're doing.
8   Vagrant.configure("2") do |config|
9     # The most common configuration options are documented and commented belo
10    # For a complete reference, please see the online documentation at
11    # https://docs.vagrantup.com.
12
13    # Every Vagrant development environment requires a box. You can search fo
14    # boxes at https://vagrantcloud.com/search.
15    config.vm.box = "base
16
17    # Disable automatic box update checking. If you disable this, then
18    # boxes will only be checked for updates when the user runs
19    # `vagrant box outdated`. This is not recommended.
20    # config.vm.box_check_update = false
21
22    # Create a forwarded port mapping which allows access to a specific port
23    # within the machine from a port on the host machine. In the example belo
24    # accessing "localhost:8080" will access port 80 on the guest machine.
25    # NOTE: This will enable public access to the opened port
26    # config.vm.network "forwarded_port", guest: 80, host: 8080
```

Looking at line 24, we can see the value `# accessing "localhost:8080" will access port 80 on` mentioned in the error. Now, although this is a comment, we can see that the `localhost:8080` value is exposed because it is wrapped in double quotes ("). If we trace back towards the beginning of the file, we should come across line 15, which looks a little odd. Here, we can see the value is `config.vm.box = "base` but there is no closing double quote.

So, let's add a double quote to the end of this line, save the file, and run the `vagrant validate` command:

```
[vagrantfiletest] vagrant validate
==> vagrant: A new version of Vagrant is available: 2.1.1!
==> vagrant: To upgrade visit: https://www.vagrantup.com/downloads.html

Vagrantfile validated successfully.
```

Great! As you can see in the preceding screenshot, we have successfully found the error and fixed it.

Summary

In this chapter, we looked at how to configure Vagrant using the Vagrantfile. We also looked at various parts of the Vagrantfile, such as how to create one, its supported commands, options, and values, its syntax and layout, and how to troubleshoot it when there is an issue. In the coming chapters, we will be using the Vagrantfile more to focus on specific areas of Vagrant, such as provisioning.

In Chapter 6, *Networking in Vagrant*, we will look at networking in Vagrant. In it, we will learn about the three main types of networking configurations: port-forwarding, public networks, and private networks.

Networking in Vagrant

6

In this chapter, we will be focusing on networking in Vagrant. By the end of this chapter, you will have a good understanding of the different networking options available in Vagrant. You will be able to configure networking in Vagrant using simple methods, such as port-forwarding, or set custom IP addresses using public and private networking.

Here are the three networking types present in Vagrant that you will learn about in this chapter:

- Port-forwarding
- Private networking
- Public networking

Port-forwarding

A powerful yet simple way to configure networking in Vagrant is to use port-forwarding. This does not require any advanced knowledge or configuration on your part.

Port-forwarding is the action of linking a port on your host machine to a port on the guest machine. It is as simple as that, but can be really powerful as it allows you to get up and running quickly.

The following are the steps to configure port-forwarding:

1. Open up our Vagrantfile. We'll start with a very basic Vagrantfile by using the `ubuntu/xenial64` box and a basic shell provision script to install the nginx web server:

```ruby
# -*- mode: ruby -*-
# vi: set ft=ruby :

Vagrant.configure("2") do |config|

  config.vm.box = "ubuntu/xenial64"

  config.vm.provision "shell", inline: <<-SHELL
    apt-get update
    apt-get install -y nginx
  SHELL
end
```

2. Once you've saved the Vagrantfile, run the `vagrant up` command:

```
[vagrant-networking] vagrant up
Bringing machine 'default' up with 'virtualbox' provider...
==> default: Importing base box 'ubuntu/xenial64'...
```

3. Once the box has completed installing nginx and is up and running, open your web browser and try navigating to `localhost:8080`:

4. nginx should be available (possibly not on `port 8080`), but as you can see, we cannot access it. This is because we have not yet set up port-forwarding. If we access localhost from inside the Vagrant machine, we should be able to access it.

5. Run the `vagrant ssh` command. Once in the Vagrant machine, run the `curl localhost` command. This should return the nginx default page in HTML code:

```
vagrant@ubuntu-xenial:~$ curl localhost
<!DOCTYPE html>
<html>
<head>
<title>Welcome to nginx!</title>
<style>
    body {
        width: 35em;
        margin: 0 auto;
        font-family: Tahoma, Verdana, Arial, sans-serif;
    }
</style>
</head>
<body>
<h1>Welcome to nginx!</h1>
<p>If you see this page, the nginx web server is successfully installed and
working. Further configuration is required.</p>

<p>For online documentation and support please refer to
<a href="http://nginx.org/">nginx.org</a>.<br/>
Commercial support is available at
<a href="http://nginx.com/">nginx.com</a>.</p>

<p><em>Thank you for using nginx.</em></p>
</body>
```

6. Let's set up port forwarding so we can access this page from the host machine (outside Vagrant).

7. Exit out of the machine and open up your Vagrantfile again. In the following code (you can see it on line 8 of the following screenshot) – `config.vm.network "forwarded_port", guest: 80, host: 8080`:

```ruby
# -*- mode: ruby -*-
# vi: set ft=ruby :

Vagrant.configure("2") do |config|

  config.vm.box = "ubuntu/xenial64"

  config.vm.network "forwarded_port", guest: 80, host: 8080

  config.vm.provision "shell", inline: <<-SHELL
    apt-get update
    apt-get install -y nginx
  SHELL
end
```

Let's break down the line that we just added into the Vagrantfile. First of all, we are calling the `config.vm.network` namespace to tell Vagrant that we want to change the network settings. The first argument we are passing in is `forwarded_port`, followed by two different port numbers. The first port is the port number that we will be accessing inside the guest/Vagrant machine. In the preceding example, we will be accessing port 80, which is generally the default port for a website/web server. The final argument is the host port, which is the port that we connect to from our host. In our example, it would be `8080`, and via URL we could access it at `http://localhost:8080`, which would connect to Vagrant and access the machine's `port 80`.

8. Save the Vagranfile and run the `vagrant reload --provision` command.

9. This will restart the Vagrant machine and force provisioning to run again. You'll see, at the bottom of the following screenshot, that it now includes our new port in the `default: Forwarding ports...` section:

```
[vagrant-networking] vagrant reload --provision
==> default: Attempting graceful shutdown of VM...
==> default: Checking if box 'ubuntu/xenial64' is up to date...
==> default: A newer version of the box 'ubuntu/xenial64' for provider 'virtualb
ox' is
==> default: available! You currently have version '20180510.0.0'. The latest is
 version
==> default: '20180622.0.0'. Run `vagrant box update` to update.
==> default: Clearing any previously set forwarded ports...
==> default: Clearing any previously set network interfaces...
==> default: Preparing network interfaces based on configuration...
    default: Adapter 1: nat
==> default: Forwarding ports...
    default: 80 (guest) => 8080 (host) (adapter 1)
    default: 22 (guest) => 2222 (host) (adapter 1)
```

10. Once the Vagrant machine is finished provisioning and is up and running, try to open `localhost:8080` in your browser:

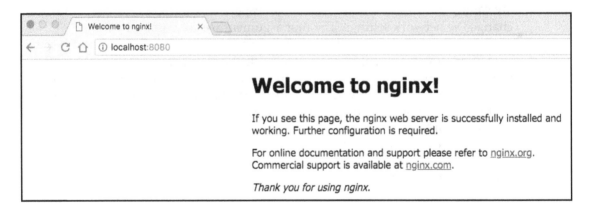

You should see the **Welcome to nginx!** default page. Congratulations! You have successfully configured port-forwarding on your Vagrant box.

Port-forwarding notes

When using the port-forwarding option within the Vagrantfile, there are a few tips you can use.

If you wish to forward multiple ports, simply create a new line and add the new guest/host ports. This could get messy if you have lots of ports to manage. At this point, it may be worth looking into the public and private networking options later in this chapter.

There are more options/parameters that you can use with this configuration:

- `auto_correct`: Used for port-collision. If set to `true`, Vagrant will check to see whether it collides with a port already being used. If one is found, Vagrant will change the port number automatically.
- `guest_ip`: The IP address of the guest that you wish to bind to the forwarded port.
- `host_ip`: The IP address of the host that you wish to bind to the forwarded port.
- `protocol`: The protocol allowed through the forwarded port. You may supply `udp` or `tcp` as options.
- `id`: The rule name visible in VirtualBox. This would be formatted as *[protocol][guest]*, for example `udp111`.

These arguments are optional. However, you are required to specify the `guest` and `host` port values.

Private networking

Private networking allows your Vagrant machine to be assigned and accessed via a private address space IP address. An example of a private IP address would be one you may have seen on your local area network, such as `192.168.1.2`.

Using this method can enable less restriction when accessing your Vagrant machine compared to port forwarding, since, by default, you can access any available port on that local IP address.

To use private networking, there are two main options. You can allow the IP address to be assigned by the **Dynamic Host Configuration Protocol** (**DHCP**) or you can choose one manually by adding in a static IP address.

DHCP

Follow these step to use the DHCP option:

1. You must select `dhcp` as the value for the `type` parameter. Within your Vagrantfile, add the following line to enable DHCP private networking:

    ```
    config.vm.network "private_network", type: "dhcp"
    ```

2. When you save the Vagrantfile, you can run `vagrant up --provision` to see the changes:

    ```
    ➡ default: Clearing any previously set forwarded ports...
    ➡ default: Clearing any previously set network interfaces...
    ➡ default: Preparing network interfaces based on configuration...
        default: Adapter 1: nat
        default: Adapter 2: hostonly
    ```

3. To find out the IP address of the newly-upped Vagrant machine, we must SSH into the machine itself.

4. Run the `vagrant ssh` command. Once in the Vagrant machine, run the `ifconfig` command (this networking command will depend on the operating system). Here is an example output:

    ```
    vagrant@ubuntu-xenial:~$ ifconfig
    enp0s3    Link encap:Ethernet  HWaddr 02:41:7b:83:f1:96
              inet addr:10.0.2.15  Bcast:10.0.2.255  Mask:255.255.255.0
              inet6 addr: fe80::41:7bff:fe83:f196/64 Scope:Link
              UP BROADCAST RUNNING MULTICAST  MTU:1500  Metric:1
              RX packets:982 errors:0 dropped:0 overruns:0 frame:0
              TX packets:573 errors:0 dropped:0 overruns:0 carrier:0
              collisions:0 txqueuelen:1000
              RX bytes:386087 (386.0 KB)  TX bytes:73933 (73.9 KB)

    enp0s8    Link encap:Ethernet  HWaddr 08:00:27:16:6e:1a
              inet addr:172.28.128.3  Bcast:172.28.128.255  Mask:255.255.255.0
              inet6 addr: fe80::a00:27ff:fe16:6e1a/64 Scope:Link
              UP BROADCAST RUNNING MULTICAST  MTU:1500  Metric:1
              RX packets:2 errors:0 dropped:0 overruns:0 frame:0
              TX packets:10 errors:0 dropped:0 overruns:0 carrier:0
              collisions:0 txqueuelen:1000
              RX bytes:1180 (1.1 KB)  TX bytes:1332 (1.3 KB)
    ```

5. In the `enp0s8` section, you can see there is a red underlined value starting with `inet addr:`. This is the private IP address that our Vagrant machine is using. The value is `172.28.128.3`. Let's see whether we can now access the machine via this IP address.

6. Open an internet browser on your host machine and type in the IP address that was returned inside your Vagrant machine.

> You should still have nginx running on `port 80` inside the Vagrant machine to see the results.

7. The following is an example of me navigating to that private IP address and seeing the nginx web server default page that was served from inside the Vagrant machine:

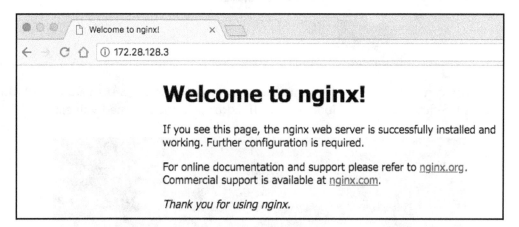

Static IP

To use the static IP option:

1. Enter a private address space IP address as the value for the `ip` parameter. Within your Vagrantfile, add the following line to enable static IP private networking:

```
config.vm.network "private_network", ip: "10.10.10.10"
```

2. When you save the Vagrantfile, run `vagrant up --provision` to force the changes. To confirm that your changes have been made, enter the `10.10.10.10` IP address into your internet browser on your host machine to see whether you get the nginx homepage:

3. You can also `vagrant ssh` into the machine, run the `ifconfig` command (this is OS-dependant), and look for that IP address in the returned values:

```
vagrant@ubuntu-xenial:~$ ifconfig
enp0s3    Link encap:Ethernet  HWaddr 02:41:7b:83:f1:96
          inet addr:10.0.2.15  Bcast:10.0.2.255  Mask:255.255.255.0
          inet6 addr: fe80::41:7bff:fe83:f196/64 Scope:Link
          UP BROADCAST RUNNING MULTICAST  MTU:1500  Metric:1
          RX packets:1213 errors:0 dropped:0 overruns:0 frame:0
          TX packets:745 errors:0 dropped:0 overruns:0 carrier:0
          collisions:0 txqueuelen:1000
          RX bytes:420984 (420.9 KB)  TX bytes:91167 (91.1 KB)

enp0s8    Link encap:Ethernet  HWaddr 08:00:27:74:8d:fe
          inet addr:10.10.10.10  Bcast:10.10.10.255  Mask:255.255.255.0
          inet6 addr: fe80::a00:27ff:fe74:8dfe/64 Scope:Link
          UP BROADCAST RUNNING MULTICAST  MTU:1500  Metric:1
          RX packets:20 errors:0 dropped:0 overruns:0 frame:0
          TX packets:28 errors:0 dropped:0 overruns:0 carrier:0
          collisions:0 txqueuelen:1000
          RX bytes:1524 (1.5 KB)  TX bytes:1848 (1.8 KB)
```

4. When using the (static IP) option with private networking, there is an optional parameter you can supply. The `auto_config` parameter allows you to enable or disable auto-configuration. If you wish to manually configure the network interface, you can disable it using the `false` value:

```
config.vm.network "private_network", ip: "10.10.10.10",
auto_config: false
```

I've found that in certain circumstances, sometimes you have to disable `auto_config` to get the static IP address to work.

IPv6

You can also specify an IPv6 address using a similar format in your Vagrantfile:

```
config.vm.network "private_network", ip: "fd12:3456:789a:1::1"
```

Using an IPv6 address is not supported by the DHCP option and must be supported by your host machine/network adapter. It is worth mentioning that the default subnet for IPv6 is `/64`.

Public networking

Public networking in Vagrant can be quite a confusing concept. In essence, it is private networking, but Vagrant will attempt to allow public access from outside your host machine (if your provider and machine will allow it) instead of just allowing access from inside the host machine.

By performing the following steps, you should be able to access your Vagrant machine via an IP address from another device on your local network. Make sure that you have nginx installed so you know when you have successfully connected via HTTP to the IP address. I have been able to view the nginx default page using my smartphone on the same local network. If you were to use the `private_networking` option, this would not work and my smartphone would not be able to load a page or find the device, which would result in a timeout.

There are two main ways to set up public networking: you can use DHCP or manually assign a static IP address.

DHCP

The fastest and easiest way to get started with public networking is to allow DHCP to assign an IP address to the Vagrant machine:

1. In your Vagrantfile, use `config.vm.network "public_network"` to get it started.

> There is no need to specify the `type` parameter like you would in the private networking DHCP configuration.

2. Run the `vagrant up --provision` command to get the Vagrant machine up and running. As we are using a public network, you will be prompted to select a bridged network interface. Depending on your requirements and some possible trial and error, choose one. I will select the first option, `1) en0: (Wi-Fi) Airport`:

```
==> default: Clearing any previously set forwarded ports...
==> default: Clearing any previously set network interfaces...
==> default: Available bridged network interfaces:
1) en0: Wi-Fi (AirPort)
2) en1: Thunderbolt 1
3) p2p0
4) awdl0
5) bridge0
==> default: When choosing an interface, it is usually the one that is
==> default: being used to connect to the internet.
    default: Which interface should the network bridge to?
```

3. To find out the IP address of the newly-upped Vagrant machine, we must SSH into the machine itself. Run the `vagrant ssh` command. Once in the Vagrant machine, run the `ifconfig` command (this networking command will depend on the operating system).

   There is an optional parameter that can be supplied when using DHCP. This is the *DHCP assigned default route*. In certain cases, this option may be required.

4. An example of this parameter would be adding `config.vm.network "public_network", use_dhcp_assigned_default_route: true` into your Vagrantfile.

Static IP

Configuring a static IP address of your choice with public networking is fairly straightforward. You must supply the `ip` parameter in the Vagrantfile and add in the IP address you wish to use. Here is an example of the configuration in my Vagrantfile:

```
config.vm.network "public_network", ip: "192.168.1.123"
```

Save your Vagrantfile and run the `vagrant up --provision` command to get the Vagrant machine up and running. As we are using a public network, you will be prompted to select a bridged network interface. Depending on your requirements and some possible trial and error then choose one. I will select the first option, `1) en0: (Wi-Fi) Airport:`

```
==> default: Clearing any previously set forwarded ports...
==> default: Clearing any previously set network interfaces...
==> default: Available bridged network interfaces:
1) en0: Wi-Fi (AirPort)
2) en1: Thunderbolt 1
3) p2p0
4) awdl0
5) bridge0
==> default: When choosing an interface, it is usually the one that is
==> default: being used to connect to the internet.
    default: Which interface should the network bridge to? █
```

Network bridge

As you've seen in the public network DHCP and static IP address, when you run the `vagrant up` or `vagrant up --provision` command, you will be asked to select which network bridge to use. To avoid this step, you can supply the default network bridge in the Vagrantfile as an additional parameter: `config.vm.network "public_network", bridge: "en0: Wi-Fi (AirPort)"`.

Summary

In this chapter, we looked at how to configure and manage networking in Vagrant. We focused on the three main types available: port-forwarding, private networking, and public networking. You should now be able to configure Vagrant to match your networking needs.

In Chapter 7, *Multi-Machine*, we'll look at Vagrant's multi-machine feature. This cool feature allows us to configure and provision multiple Vagrant machines from one Vagrantfile config. We'll create a real-world scenario of having multiple Vagrant machines – one will act as a load balancer that distributes HTTP traffic between two Vagrant boxes and a web server.

7
Multi-Machine

In this chapter, you will learn about Vagrant's multi-machine feature. We will walk through various aspects of multi-machine, and by the end of this chapter you should have a good understanding of the following topics:

- An introduction to Vagrant multi-machine
- Multi-machine configuration in the Vagrantfile
- Connecting multi-machines via networking

An introduction to Vagrant multi-machine

Using Vagrant's multi-machine feature, you can easily manage multiple Vagrant machines in one Vagrantfile. This can be useful if you wish to model your test environment in a similar way to your production environment. You can easily separate servers such as web servers, file servers, and database servers.

In this section, we will look at using multi-machine in the two following use cases:

- In the first use case, we will look at managing three Vagrant machines. Here, we will create a basic load balancing setup, where one machine will distribute traffic between two machines that serve up a website.
- In the second use case, we will be managing two Vagrant machines. We will create a web-based machine that serves a website and another machine, which runs a MySQL database. The web machine will communicate with the database machine to display data on the web page.

Load balancing with Vagrant multi-machine

In this section, we are going to be using nginx to act as an HTTP load balancer that will distribute traffic between two nginx web machines. We will be using the round robin method of load balancing, which evenly distributes incoming traffic.

First, let's set up our Vagrantfile to contain the three machines before installing nginx with the Ubuntu 16.04 64-bit OS.

To get started, let's create a minimal Vagrantfile by running the `vagrant init -m` command. After that, let's edit the Vagrantfile and create three config areas as follows:

```
Vagrant.configure("2") do |config|
    # Configure load balancer machine
    config.vm.define "lb1" do |lb1|
    end
    # Configure first web machine
    config.vm.define "web1" do |web1|
    end
    # Configure second web machine
    config.vm.define "web2" do |web2|
    end
end
```

Our Vagrantfile should now have the main `|config|` block, which encapsulates all of the code and the three `define` blocks within that. Multi-machine is incredibly easy to set up in Vagrant; all you have to do is define a new machine and then configure that machine within the block.

When defining a new block you must give the new machine a name that will become its reference during configuration. The first machine I have set up is named `lb1`, which simply stands for load balancer 1. This convention can help when working with a large Vagrantfile and multiple machines; it can also be useful when working on a team where multiple developers are using and viewing a Vagrantfile.

To define a new machine, input the following two lines of code:

```
config.vm.define "lb1" do |lb1|
end
```

This machine is now ready to configure! If we run `vagrant up`, nothing will happen because the box has no values – there is no box, networking, provisioning, or file handling defined.

Let's start configuring our load balancer machine by setting a box and an IP address. This can be done by accessing the `lb1` namespace within our config block, as follows:

```
config.vm.define "lb1" do |lb1|
    lb1.vm.box = "ubuntu/xenial64"
    lb1.vm.network "private_network", ip: "10.0.0.10"
end
```

As you can see in the preceding example, we have set the `lb1.vm.box` and `lb1.vm.network` values. Let's now do this for our two web machines, but let's set a different IP address so we can access them separately and avoid conflicts, as follows:

```
config.vm.define "web1" do |web1|
    web1.vm.box = "ubuntu/xenial64"
    web1.vm.network "private_network", ip: "10.0.0.11"
end
config.vm.define "web2" do |web2|
    web2.vm.box = "ubuntu/xenial64"
    web2.vm.network "private_network", ip: "10.0.0.12"
end
```

We now have three Vagrant machines configured, but before we can launch and test them, we need to provision them with nginx and configure nginx for our load balancing setup.

Let's create two shell scripts to provision our machines. (We will cover shell scripting in more depth in later chapters; we are using it here to help demonstrate how it works within a multi-machine environment.)

In the directory where your `Vagrantfile` is, create a `lb.sh` file and an `web.sh` file.

lb.sh

Let's focus on the `lb.sh` file first. Add the following lines as the file's contents:

```
#!/bin/bash
echo 'Starting Provision: lb1'
 sudo apt-get update
 sudo apt-get install -y nginx
 sudo service nginx stop
 sudo rm -rf /etc/nginx/sites-enabled/default
 sudo touch /etc/nginx/sites-enabled/default
 echo "upstream testapp {
     server 10.0.0.11;
     server 10.0.0.12;
 }
server {
```

```
        listen 80 default_server;
        listen [::]:80 default_server ipv6only=on;
     root /usr/share/nginx/html;
        index index.html index.htm;
       # Make site accessible from http://localhost/
        server_name localhost;
     location / {
            proxy_pass http://testapp;
        }
  }" >> /etc/nginx/sites-enabled/default
   sudo service nginx start
   echo "Machine: lb1" > /var/www/html/index.html
   echo 'Provision lb1 complete'
```

There's quite a bit going on in the preceding snippet, so let's break it down.

In the first part, we are declaring the program location that should run this script (bin/bash) after the shebang (#!).

In lines 2-7, we are updating Ubuntu, installing nginx, and deleting the default nginx configuration file.

In lines 8-22, we are inserting a new config as the default nginx config, which essentially setes up the load balancing and sets our available web servers as 10.0.0.11 and 10.0.0.12.

In lines 23-25, we are starting up the nginx service (which will read our new default config file and apply those settings), setting up the default index HTML file, and finishing the provision.

We echo out Starting Provision: lb1 and Provision lb1 complete at both the beginning and end of the provision script. This is not necessary, but when you run the vagrant up --provision command you will see these echoed into the terminal, which can be useful when you are trying to understand what is happening and what stage of the provision process you are at.

web.sh

Let's now create our web.sh bash script, which will handle the provisioning of our web servers. This script is much simpler than the load balancer script we created earlier, as follows:

```
#!/bin/bash
echo 'Starting Provision: web'$1
 sudo apt-get update
```

```
sudo apt-get install -y nginx
echo "<h1>Machine: web"$1 "</h1>" > /var/www/html/index.html
echo 'Provision web'$1 'complete'
```

Again, in the preceding snippet, we are echoing out the progress at the beginning and end of our provision progress. In lines 2-4 we are updating Ubuntu and installing nginx. In line 5 we are overwriting the default index HTML file with a basic title, which will help us differentiate between the two web servers.

In this script you will notice the use of $1. This is a variable in bash and references the first argument. Later on in this section you will learn how to pass an argument into the shell script, as this will help us differentiate between web server 1 and web server 2.

Vagrant multi-machine shell provisioning

Now that we have our lb.sh and web.sh provisioning scripts set up, let's add them into our Vagrantfile so we're ready to set up and test our load balancing app.

The following code block is a finished copy of our Vagrantfile:

```
Vagrant.configure("2") do |config|
    # Configure load balancer machine
    config.vm.define "lb1" do |lb1|
        lb1.vm.box = "ubuntu/xenial64"
        lb1.vm.network "private_network", ip: "10.0.0.10"
        lb1.vm.provision :shell do |shell|
            shell.path = "lb.sh"
        end
    end
    # Configure first web machine
    config.vm.define "web1" do |web1|
        web1.vm.box = "ubuntu/xenial64"
        web1.vm.network "private_network", ip: "10.0.0.11"
        web1.vm.provision :shell do |shell|
            shell.args = "1"
            shell.path = "web.sh"
        end
    end
    # Configure second web machine
    config.vm.define "web2" do |web2|
        web2.vm.box = "ubuntu/xenial64"
        web2.vm.network "private_network", ip: "10.0.0.12"
        web2.vm.provision :shell do |shell|
            shell.args = "2"
            shell.path = "web.sh"
        end
```

```
        end
    end
```

We can provision a box by using the `.vm.provision` namespace. In the preceding example, you can see that we are passing our arguments into `web1` and `web2` using the `shell.args` value. These will then be accessible inside our `web.sh` script.

Now, save your Vagrantfile and run the `vagrant up --provision` command to start running and provisioning the machines. You'll notice that the booting process takes much longer as there are now three machines to manage instead of the usual one.

During the booting process you should notice our echo statements at different points of the provisioning process, as shown in the following screenshots:

In the preceding screenshot, you'll see the `lb1` provisioner has started. In the following screenshot you'll see that the `web2` provisioner has completed:

When the Vagrant machines have finished booting, we can move on and test out the load balancer. To do this, we set the IP address for the load balancer to `10.0.0.10` and open it in a browser. You should see one of the web server machines, as shown in the following screenshot:

Now, if you refresh the page, the load balancer should send your request to the other web server machine, as shown in the following screenshot:

If you keep refreshing the page, you will be bounced between the two web servers. You can also go to one of the web machines directly be accessing them via their own IP addresses. If you visit 10.0.0.11 in your web browser, for example, you will only see the web server 1 machine, as shown in the following screenshot:

Congratulations! You have successfully configured a multi-machine Vagrant environment using a basic HTTP load balancing setup.

multi-machine SSH

Now that your machines are up and running, you may want to SSH into them to make and test some changes. To do this, we can run the vagrant ssh command. This will give us an error, as shown in the following screenshot:

```
[multi-machine] vagrant ssh
This command requires a specific VM name to target in a multi-VM environment.
```

Here, we must specify a machine name, otherwise the ssh command won't know which machine we want to connect to. The names to supply are the ones we defined in the Vagrantfile, for example, lb1, web1, or web2. Let's now SSH into the load balancing machine by running the vagrant ssh lb1 command, as follows:

```
[multi-machine] vagrant ssh lb1
Welcome to Ubuntu 16.04.4 LTS (GNU/Linux 4.4.0-124-generic x86_64)
```

You can now manage each machine individually via SSH.

Let's complete the machine life cycle by halting and destroying the machines. We can halt all three machines by running the `vagrant halt` command, as shown in the following screenshot:

```
[multi-machine] vagrant halt
==> web2: Attempting graceful shutdown of VM...
==> web1: Attempting graceful shutdown of VM...
==> lb1: Attempting graceful shutdown of VM...
```

Next, if you wish to do so, you can destroy your machines to free up system memory. Run the `vagrant destroy -f` command. In our example, we are using the `-f` flag to force the machines' destruction; otherwise, we will be prompted for confirmation for each machine. Run the following command:

```
[multi-machine] vagrant destroy -f
==> web2: Destroying VM and associated drives...
==> web1: Destroying VM and associated drives...
==> lb1: Destroying VM and associated drives...
```

As you can see in the preceding screenshot, the command tells Vagrant to loop through each machine and destroy them.

Web server and database setup with Vagrant multi-machine

In this section, we will use Vagrant's multi-machine feature to create a traditional web server and database setup. We will install our web server (nginx and PHP) on one machine and our database server (MySQL) on another.

This setup is simpler than the one in the previous section, but it should still help to reinforce how to set up and manage Vagrant multi-machine.

First, let's create a new Vagrantfile in a new folder. We will create two machines to get started, as follows:

```
Vagrant.configure("2") do |config|
    # Configure web server machine
    config.vm.define "web1" do |web1|
        web1.vm.box = "ubuntu/xenial64"
        web1.vm.network "private_network", ip: "10.0.0.50"
        web1.vm.provision :shell do |shell|
```

```
            shell.path = "web.sh"
        end
    end
    # Configure database server machine
    config.vm.define "db1" do |db1|
        db1.vm.box = "ubuntu/xenial64"
        db1.vm.network "private_network", ip: "10.0.0.51"
        db1.vm.provision :shell do |shell|
            shell.path = "db.sh"
        end
    end
  end
end
```

Again, we will be using shell provisioning for these machines. We will be using the Ubuntu 16.04 box with private networking, and each machine will get its own private IP address.

web.sh

Let's now create our web server provision script to install nginx and PHP. Inside the web.sh file, we input the following code:

```
#!/bin/bash
echo 'Starting Provision: web server'
 sudo apt-get update
 sudo apt-get install -y nginx
 touch /var/www/html/index.php
 sudo apt-get install -y php-fpm php-mysql
 echo 'Provision web server complete'
```

We will need to log into the machine to make some configuration changes manually, but the preceding snippet will give us a good start.

db.sh

We can now create our database server provision script to install MySQL. Inside the db.sh file, we input the following code:

```
#!/bin/bash
echo 'Starting Provision: database server'
 sudo apt-get update
 echo 'Provision database server complete'
```

This stage will also require some manual configuration, which we can do by logging into the database machine.

Let's now start up our Vagrant machines by running the `vagrant up --provision` command.

Nginx and PHP configuration

Let's now configure Nginx and PHP on our web server machine. Log into the machine by running the `vagrant ssh web1` command.

Once logged in, we need to finish configuring nginx. This can be done by editing the default config file with the following command:

```
sudo nano /etc/nginx/sites-available/default
```

We now need to add PHP into this file to allow nginx to handle PHP files and code. The first line we need to edit is the index file list, so find the following line:

```
index index.html index.htm index.nginx-debian.html;
```

Chanage it to this:

```
index index.php index.html index.htm index.nginx-debian.html;
```

The final change we need to perform is to add the PHP handling. This requires us to edit a block inside the main `server {}` block. The following snippet is the code we need to edit:

```
#location ~ \.php$ {
#       include snippets/fastcgi-php.conf;
#
#       # With php7.0-cgi alone:
#       fastcgi_pass 127.0.0.1:9000;
#       # With php7.0-fpm:
#       fastcgi_pass unix:/run/php/php7.0-fpm.sock;
#}
```

Change the preceding snippet to the following:

```
location ~ \.php$ {
        include snippets/fastcgi-php.conf;
      # With php7.0-fpm:
        fastcgi_pass unix:/run/php/php7.0-fpm.sock;
  }
```

Now save and close the file. If you want to, you can use the `sudo nginx -t` command to test the code and syntax of the config file you have just edited. A successful message is as follows:

```
vagrant@ubuntu-xenial:~$ sudo nginx -t
nginx: the configuration file /etc/nginx/nginx.conf syntax is ok
nginx: configuration file /etc/nginx/nginx.conf test is successful
```

```
sudo systemctl reload nginx
```

To confirm PHP has been installed and is working, create a `test.php` file within the `/var/www/html/` directory. Within the `test.php` file, add the following lines:

```
<?php
phpinfo();
?>
```

Save the file and in your web browser on your host machine, open `http://10.0.0.50/test.php`. You should now see the PHP info page, as shown in the following screenshot:

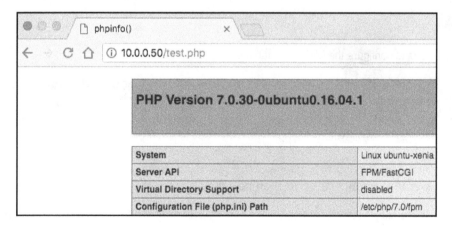

While we're here, we should go back into the `test.php` file and edit its contents. So, we are now going to create a basic PHP script that connects to our MySQL database and retrieves some data. Edit the file to contain the following snippets:

```
<?php
$conn = new mysqli("10.0.0.51", "external", "password", "VagrantDatabase");
$result = $conn->query("SELECT VagrantText FROM VagrantTable WHERE
```

```
    VagrantId = 1");
    while($row = $result->fetch_assoc()) {
        echo $row['VagrantText'];
    }
    ?>
```

 This is a very basic script to help get you started. This script is not secure and does not necessarily follow the PHP best practices. It would not be recommended to use this script in a production environment.

Before we can continue, we must set up the MySQL server on our other Vagrant machine; otherwise, the PHP script will fail as there is no database available.

MySQL configuration

Let's finish our setup by installing and configuring the MySQL database. At the end of this section, you should see the final working code, as well as your web server accessing the database server via PHP.

 It is not recommended to use this setup in a production environment. We are not following security best practices but are instead setting things up with basic configuration.

Follow these steps to configure the MySQL database:

1. First, let's SSH into the database machine by running the `vagrant ssh db1` command.
2. Now install MySQL by running the following command: `run sudo apt-get install mysql-server`.

You'll now be asked to set a root password. This can be anything as we are not using this as a production environment. You will then be asked to repeat and confirm the root password.

You can now log into MySQL via the terminal by running `mysql -u root -p`. Enter the root password that you just set.

We must now create a basic MySQL user that has the correct privileges to access the database outside of the localhost address and network. Without this, we would not be able to access the database from the web1 machine, so run the following commands:

```
CREATE USER 'external'@'localhost' IDENTIFIED BY 'password';
GRANT ALL PRIVILEGES ON *.* TO 'external'@'localhost' WITH GRANT OPTION;
CREATE USER 'external'@'%' IDENTIFIED BY 'password';
GRANT ALL PRIVILEGES ON *.* TO 'external'@'%' WITH GRANT OPTION;
FLUSH PRIVILEGES;
```

We can now create a table and enter some test data, which will be accessed via PHP on the web1 machine. Run the following commands to create a new database, a new table, and insert some data:

```
CREATE DATABASE VagrantDatabase;
USE VagrantDatabase;
CREATE TABLE VagrantTable (VagrantId int, VagrantText varchar(255));
INSERT INTO VagrantTable (VagrantId, VagrantText) VALUES (1, "This text is
from MySQL");
```

You can now exit the MySQL CLI tool. We must now configure one last MySQL setting that will allow connections from our web1 machine. We need to edit the mysqld.cnf config file, which can be done by running the following command:

```
sudo nano /etc/mysql/mysql.conf.d/mysqld.cnf
```

Look for the following line:

```
bind_address = 127.0.0.1
```

Change it to the following:

```
bind_address = 0.0.0.0
```

You can now save the file and run the following command. This will restart MySQL so it is using the new configuration:

```
sudo service mysql restart
```

We can now exit the MySQL CLI and visit `http://10.0.0.50/test.php` to access our database, as shown in the following screenshot:

Congratulations! You have successfully set up Vagrant multi-machine so it uses two machines as a web server and database architecture.

Summary

In this chapter, we learned about Vagrant's multi-machine feature and created two use cases: load balancing with three machines and a web server and database architecture with two machines.

In `Chapter 8`, *Exploring Vagrant Plugins and Syncing Files*, we will learn about Vagrant plugins and how to sync files between a host machine and a Vagrant guest machine.

Exploring Vagrant Plugins and Syncing Files

8

In this chapter, we will cover powerful, additional functionality in Vagrant. We will learn about Vagrant plugins and syncing files between the host machine and guest machine. By the end of this chapter, you will have a good understanding of the following:

- Understanding Vagrant plugins
- Managing Vagrant plugins
- Vagrant plugin commands and subcommands
- Finding, installing, and using a Vagrant plugin
- Vagrant file syncing
- Syncing files – shared folders, Rsync, and NFS

Understanding Vagrant plugins

Vagrant provides many options and features, but when you require something that isn't available, you can extend this functionality in the form of a plugin. Vagrant provides a powerful and robust internal API that is easy to use and flexible to develop with. Vagrant actually uses its own API for many core features.

The anatomy of a Vagrant plugin

There are multiple parts of a Vagrant plugin. Some parts are for development and others are for the general use of the plugin. We'll focus on two core elements: **gem** and **bundler**.

Gem

A gem is a specific file written in Ruby that uses the `.gem` file extension. A gem is made up of three parts: the code that includes the logic, tests, and utilities; documentation; and a gemspec that includes information about the author and other metadata. The gem file is the core part of the Vagrant plugin and is the code that is run when you use the plugin in your Vagrant machine.

bundler

bundler is an application that Vagrant uses and interfaces with to manage the plugin and plugin dependencies. It is often used in Ruby projects to manage gems and gem versioning. You will often see bundler's output in the console when an installation of a vagrant plugin fails. Because Vagrant plugins are written in Ruby and saved as a gem file, using bundler is a great choice.

Managing Vagrant plugins

In this section, we will cover general plugin management, including installation and uninstallation. The most useful command when managing a Vagrant plugin is the `list` command. Run the following command to view what plugins you have installed on your system:

```
vagrant plugin list
```

There is a chance that you do not have any plugins installed and you will see a `No plugins installed` message. If you do have a plugin installed, then you will see a list similar to the following:

```
[vagrant-plugins-sync] vagrant plugin list
vagrant-hostsupdater (1.1.1.160)
```

Vagrant plugin installation methods

To start using a plugin with Vagrant, you must first install it on your system. There are currently two ways to install a plugin: you can use a local file or a gem source. Let's explore both options.

Installing a Vagrant plugin from a local file

Installing a plugin from a local source is fairly quick and easy. You may have a local file because you have developed the plugin yourself or have been given this plugin code privately by a friend or from your company.

The local file will use the .gem extension. To install the plugin, you must know the location relative to the folder that you want it to be installed/used in. I'm going to install the plugin, which is called testplugin.gem and can be found in my test-plugin folder within my current Vagrant project directory. Here is an example of the command:

```
vagrant plugin install /test-plugin/testplugin.gem
```

Vagrant and the bundler will now attempt to locate and install the plugin. If it cannot be found, you will receive the following error message:

```
Bundler, the underlying system Vagrant uses to install plugins,
reported an error. The error is shown below. These errors are usually
caused by misconfigured plugin installations or transient network
issues. The error from Bundler is:

No such file or directory @ rb_sysopen - /test-plugin/testplugin.gem
```

If there is a problem with the plugin, such as a syntax error in the gem file, you will see a message similar to this:

```
[vagrant-plugins-sync] vagrant plugin install testmyplugintest
Installing the 'testmyplugintest' plugin. This can take a few minutes...
Bundler, the underlying system Vagrant uses to install plugins,
reported an error. The error is shown below. These errors are usually
caused by misconfigured plugin installations or transient network
issues. The error from Bundler is:

Unable to resolve dependency: user requested 'testmyplugintest (> 0)'
```

Installing a Vagrant plugin from a known gem source

The second way to install a plugin is from a known gem source. A known gem source is a remote repository that the bundler system will attempt to locate and install a gem from. The most popular gem source is RubyGems, which is a ruby gem-hosting service.

Let's install a new plugin via this method. Here is an example command to run:

```
vagrant plugin install vagrant-hostsupdater
```

You will learn more about installing plugins and managing plugins in the coming sections.

Vagrant plugin commands and subcommands

The `plugin` command within Vagrant offers a number of commands and subcommands. We have covered these in `Chapter 7`, *Multi-Machine*, but we'll use this as a basic reference and reminder.

You can view a list of plugin commands by running the `vagrant plugin help` command. Let's dive a little deeper into each available plugin subcommand:

- To remove all user-installed plugins and plugin data, run the `vagrant plugin expunge` command.
- To install a plugin, run the `vagrant plugin install` command. Additional parameters are required and can be seen by running the `vagrant plugin install -h` command.
- To install a license for a proprietary vagrant plugin, run the `vagrant plugin license` command. Additional parameters are required and can be seen by running the `vagrant plugin license -h` command.
- To view a list of vagrant plugins installed, run the `vagrant plugin list` command.
- To try to repair a broken plugin/issue during installation, run the `vagrant plugin repair` command.
- To uninstall a vagrant plugin, run the `vagrant plugin uninstall` command. Additional parameters are required and can be seen by running the `vagrant plugin uninstall -h` command.
- To update a vagrant plugin, run the `vagrant plugin update` command. Additional parameters are required and can be seen by running the `vagrant plugin update -h` command.

In further sections, we will use these commands in more real-world scenarios and learn how to interact with vagrant plugins.

Finding, installing, and using a Vagrant plugin

In this section, we will learn how to find, instal, and use a Vagrant plugin. This will give you a good understanding of the Vagrant plugin ecosystem and some tips to find a good plugin.

There is no official repository or website for listing Vagrant plugins (such as the Vagrant cloud for Vagrant boxes), but there are a few websites you can use to help you find that perfect plugin:

- RubyGems (`https://rubygems.org/`)
- GitHub (`https://github.com/`)
- Search engines
- Community-updated GitHub that lists popular plugins (`https://github.com/hashicorp/vagrant/wiki/Available-Vagrant-Plugins`)

RubyGems and GitHub are both code-hosting-based websites and offer powerful search facilities. I've found Google to be very useful when searching for plugins. Try using different search terms to find a plugin that matches your requirements. An example would be `vagrant plugin dns` or `vagrant dns plugins` if I were looking for a plugin to manage or interact with DNS in Vagrant.

Installing a Vagrant plugin

Let's install a plugin from the RubyGems website. I've searched for `vagrant` and found one called **vagrant-hostsupdater**, which is currently version `1.1.1.160` and has just over 500,000 downloads. Here is a screenshot of the plugin in the RubyGems search results:

---

vagrant-hostsupdater   1.1.1.160

Enables Vagrant to update hosts file on the host machine

411,701

DOWNLOADS

This plugin will attempt to edit your `/etc/hosts` file by adding and removing hosts when Vagrant machines are created and destroyed, respectively. This means that you can access the Vagrant machine by a domain name such as `machine.dev` instead of `192.168.10.10`.

We can install this plugin by running the following command:

```
vagrant plugin install vagrant-hostsupdater
```

You should see an output similar to this:

```
[vagrant-plugins-sync] vagrant plugin install vagrant-hostsupdater
Installing the 'vagrant-hostsupdater' plugin. This can take a few minutes...
Fetching: vagrant-hostsupdater-1.1.1.160.gem (100%)
Installed the plugin 'vagrant-hostsupdater (1.1.1.160)'!
```

We can verify that this has been installed by running the `vagrant plugin list` command as shown here:

```
[vagrant-plugins-sync] vagrant plugin list
vagrant-hostsupdater (1.1.1.160)
```

Let's now use and test our Vagrant plugin. This specific plugin is configured in the Vagrantfile, so let's create a basic one to get started:

1. Run the `vagrant init -m` command.
2. Edit your Vagrantfile to include the following code:

```
Vagrant.configure("2") do |config|
  config.vm.box = "ubuntu/xenial64"
  config.vm.network :private_network, ip: "192.168.100.23"
  config.vm.hostname = "vagrant.dev"
  config.vm.provision "shell", inline: <<-SHELL
    sudo apt-get update
    sudo apt-get install -y nginx
  SHELL
end
```

We create a basic Vagrant machine to test our plugin. The main lines we are concerned with are the `config.vm.network` and `config.vm.hostname` lines as they are required by our plugin.

We have created a Ubuntu machine that uses a private static IP address, the hostname of `vagrant.dev`, and a basic shell provisioner to update the system and then install the nginx web server. This will allow us to quickly and easily see that everything has worked as nginx has a default page available on port 80 once it's been installed and is running.

3. Run the `vagrant up --provision` command to get the box up and running.

You should now see a message from the [vagrant-hostsupdater] plugin, which will attempt to enter the machine's IP address and host name into the /etc/hosts file. The hosts file is an important system file and requires root permission to edit. You will be asked for the root password for your host machine:

```
==> default: [vagrant-hostsupdater] Checking for host entries
==> default: [vagrant-hostsupdater] Writing the following entries to (/etc/hosts
)
==> default: [vagrant-hostsupdater]   192.168.100.23  vagrant.dev  # VAGRANT: 9b
a6ee973a0cc55ce8fb75000d95a1dd (default) / 12b6d3ad-5975-41a6-9d43-0f0822a0d5a5
==> default: [vagrant-hostsupdater] This operation requires administrative acces
s. You may skip it by manually adding equivalent entries to the hosts file.
Password:
```

4. To test that the plugin works, we can check the /etc/hosts file before we start up the vagrant machine. Here is a basic example. If you have edited yours before, you may see more entries:

```
##
# Host Database
#
# localhost is used to configure the loopback interface
# when the system is booting.  Do not change this entry.
##
127.0.0.1       localhost
255.255.255.255 broadcasthost
::1             localhost
```

5. Once you have entered your root password and the plugin successfully writes to the /etc/hosts file, you should see this message as part of the vagrant up process:

```
==> default: Setting hostname...
```

6. Once the machine is up and running, check out the /etc/hosts file again to see whether a new entry has been added. All new entries are added at the bottom of the file. In the following screenshot, we can see that our entry is there, the IP address is 192.168.100.23 and the hostname is vagrant.dev. The plugin has also added in a comment using the # character:

```
##
# Host Database
#
# localhost is used to configure the loopback interface
# when the system is booting.  Do not change this entry.
##
127.0.0.1       localhost
255.255.255.255 broadcasthost
::1             localhost
192.168.100.23  vagrant.dev  # VAGRANT: 9ba6ee973a0cc55ce8fb75000d95a1dd
```

7. Great! Let's now test the hostname and see what we get. While we are in the terminal, we can run the curl vagrant.dev command, which will attempt to load that URL and return the contents. We can see that the default nginx page has been returned:

```
[vagrant-plugins-sync] curl vagrant.dev
<!DOCTYPE html>
<html>
<head>
<title>Welcome to nginx!</title>
<style>
    body {
        width: 35em;
        margin: 0 auto;
        font-family: Tahoma, Verdana, Arial, sans-serif;
    }
</style>
</head>
<body>
<h1>Welcome to nginx!</h1>
<p>If you see this page, the nginx web server is successfully installed and
```

8. Ping the hostname to see whether there is a live connection, packet loss, and what sort of connection times we get. As the machine is local, the speed will be very quick (less than 1 ms) and we will see the IP address returned, which in this case is `192.168.100.23`:

```
[vagrant-plugins-sync] ping -c 4 vagrant.dev
PING vagrant.dev (192.168.100.23): 56 data bytes
64 bytes from 192.168.100.23: icmp_seq=0 ttl=64 time=0.398 ms
64 bytes from 192.168.100.23: icmp_seq=1 ttl=64 time=0.495 ms
64 bytes from 192.168.100.23: icmp_seq=2 ttl=64 time=0.708 ms
64 bytes from 192.168.100.23: icmp_seq=3 ttl=64 time=0.546 ms

--- vagrant.dev ping statistics ---
4 packets transmitted, 4 packets received, 0.0% packet loss
round-trip min/avg/max/stddev = 0.398/0.537/0.708/0.112 ms
```

9. `vagrant halt` the machine. You'll see in the terminal that the plugin will now kick into action and remove that entry from the `/etc/hosts` file. You'll need to enter the root password again:

```
[vagrant-plugins-sync] vagrant halt
==> default: Attempting graceful shutdown of VM...
==> default: [vagrant-hostsupdater] Removing hosts
Password:
```

Uninstalling a Vagrant plugin

Let's now uninstall our `vagrant-hostsupdater` plugin. We can do this by running the `vagrant plugin uninstall vagrant-hostsupdater` command. If you are unsure what the plugin is called, you can run the `vagrant plugin list` command to view a list of available plugins on your system. The plugin should now be removed, you should see the `Successfully uninstalled` message:

```
[vagrant-plugins-sync] vagrant plugin uninstall vagrant-hostsupdater
Uninstalling the 'vagrant-hostsupdater' plugin...
Successfully uninstalled vagrant-hostsupdater-1.1.1.160
```

We can also verify the plugin has been removed by running the `vagrant plugin list` command. We should see the `No plugins installed` message (as long as you do not have any other plugins installed on your system):

```
[vagrant-plugins-sync] vagrant plugin list
No plugins installed.
```

Vagrant file-syncing

Syncing files is the way of sharing files between your host machine and the guest machine running within Vagrant. It allows you to edit files on your host machine and see the changes in your guest machine or vice versa.

Vagrant calls this **synced folders** and offers five ways to do this:

- Basic syncing
- SMB
- VirtualBox
- RSync
- NFS

In this section, we will cover basic usage, RSync, and NFS.

Setting up synced folders

To get started, let's create a Vagrantfile by running the `vagrant init -m` command. We'll start with basic usage-syncing, then look at RSync, and then finish with NFS.

We'll create a file on our host system, make some changes to the contents, and then view that file within our Vagrant machine. We'll then edit the file on the Vagrant machine and view its changes on the host machine. This will prove that the file can be edited both ways via the host and the Vagrant machine.

We'll need to create and edit the `config.vm.synced_folder` setting within our Vagrantfile.

Synced folders with basic usage

The basic usage of synced folders in Vagrant is easy to get set up. We can get started with just a basic Vagrantfile:

```
Vagrant.configure("2") do |config|
    config.vm.box = "ubuntu/xenial64"
    config.vm.synced_folder ".", "/home/vagrant/files"
end
```

Let's focus on line 3. The `synced_folder` config takes two parameters. The first parameter is the folder on your host machine and the second parameter is the folder within the Vagrant machine.

In this example, we are setting the first parameter to `"."`, which is the immediate directory that the Vagrantfile is in on our host machine. In the second parameter, we are setting the folder to `"/home/vagrant/files"` on the Vagrant machine.

> The default folder on the Vagrant machine is `"/home/vagrant"`, but if we try and set this as the second parameter, we will be unable to access the Vagrant machine via SSH as an error will occur when that folder is mounted on `"/home/vagrant/.ssh/authorized_keys"` as the SSH keys cannot be uploaded and checked.

Let's now test our new folder-syncing configuration:

Run the `vagrant up --provision` command. You should see a similar output from the Vagrant machine:

```
==> default: Mounting shared folders...
    default: /home/vagrant/files => /Users/alexbraunton/Projects/vagrant-plugins-sync
```

We can now SSH into the machine to see whether the `files` folder has been created (if not already available). You can run the `ls` command to list files and folders within your current directory. You should now see the `files` folder:

```
vagrant@ubuntu-xenial:~$ ls
files
```

Let's now create a file within the `files` folder:

1. Move into the folder by running the `cd files` command
2. Create a text file by running the touch `test-file.txt` command
3. Add some content by running the `echo "Hello from Vagrant!" > test-file.txt` command

We can now exit out of the Vagrant machine by running the `exit` command. You can now search for the file within the host machine's directory. You can do this by using the terminal or a text editor. I will be using the Atom text editor.

In the following screenshot, we can see the file that we created in the directory and its contents:

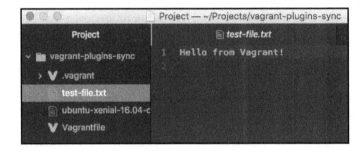

Congratulations! You have successfully configured synced folders and synced a file between your host machine and vagrant machine.

Synced folders with RSync

When using RSync as a *synced folder* option in Vagrant, it's a slightly more complex setup. RSync can be used when other options for file-syncing are not available, such as the other option we have looked at, basic usage, or in the next section, which is the NFS option.

To start using RSync, our Vagrant file just needs an extra parameter on the `config.vm.synced_folders` option:

```
config.vm.synced_folder ".", "/home/vagrant/files", type: "rsync"
```

To use this option, both the host machine and Vagrant machine must have `rsync` installed. Vagrant will attempt to install `rsync` on the Vagrant machine if possible, if not, it will display an error.

There are additional parameters available to use with the RSync option. Please view the official documentation for the most up-to-date list. These include the ability to exclude certain files.

RSync traditionally does a one-time sync from the host to guest machine unless the `rsync_auto` option is set to `true` in the Vagrantfile. This is the default value in Vagrant, but can be changed by setting the `rsync_auto` option to `false`.

Synced folders with NFS

Using NFS as a solution to syncing folders between the host and Vagrant machine can often offer performance benefits or better suit the environment you need.

Using NFS is very similar to the `basic usage` version of synced folders in Vagrant. Our Vagrant file just needs an extra parameter on the `config.vm.synced_folders` option:

```
config.vm.synced_folder ".", "/home/vagrant/files", type: "nfs"
```

We have added the `type` option with the value of `nfs`. For this to work, the OS within the Vagrant machine must support NFS.

The host machine must also support NFS by running the NFS server daemon, which is the `nfsd` package. This comes pre-installed on macOS X, but you may be required to install it if your host machine is running Linux.

Vagrant NFS-synced folders do not work on Windows hosts. If you attempt to configure this in the Vagrantfile, Vagrant will just ignore it. If you're using VirtualBox as a provider, you will also need to configure private networking when using NFS. If you are using VMWare, you don't need to worry.

Summary

In this section, we learned about two of Vagrant's main features. We looked at plugins in Vagrant and learned about what they are, how they work, and how to install/uninstall and use them. We also looked at file-syncing within Vagrant to understand how we can sync files between the host system and Vagrant machine using a number of different methods.

In Chapter 9, *Shell Scripts - Provisioning*, we will start part one of our provisioning series of chapters. We will learn about provisioning within Vagrant and how to provision a Vagrant machine using shell scripting. This will lead us into later chapters that focus on provisioning with configuration-management tools such as Chef.

Shell Scripts - Provisioning

9

In this chapter, we are going to look at Vagrant provisioning. We will focus on basic concepts and also on shell-script provisioning. By the end of this chapter, you will have a good understanding of:

- Vagrant provisioning
- Understanding configuration management
- Vagrant provisioning with a file
- Vagrant shell provisioning
- Vagrant inline scripts, external scripts, and script arguments

Introduction to Vagrant provisioning

The idea of provisioning within Vagrant is to create a script that prepares and installs software onto the Vagrant machine. Provisioning can be done inline in the Vagrantfile using a shell provisioner or external file. Provisioning happens during the *vagrant up* process as the machine is being created.

When provisioning a Vagrant machine, there are a number of options:

- Install software
- Alter configurations
- Operating-system-level changes
- System settings

Understanding configuration management

In later chapters, we will learn more about using configuration-management tools with Vagrant for provisioning. While talking about Vagrant provisioning, this will be a good introduction to configuration management.

Configuration-management tools include Chef, Ansible, and Salt. We will be focusing on these three tools. Configuration management is essentially another word for provisioning and is used to set a machine to a desired state – this could be installing software or configuring certain settings.

Configuration-management tools often have a special file type or syntax that is used. We will be focusing on the following software:

- **Ansible** (uses playbooks)
- **Chef** (uses cookbooks)
- **Docker** (uses images)
- **Puppet** (uses manifests)
- **Salt** (uses states)

Configuration management is often used when a more powerful and flexible option is needed in your development and deployment process. A benefit of using configuration-management tools is the separation of concerns. Essentially, you don't rely on Vagrant to handle too much during the process in case you have any issues or you want the flexibility of being able to change which configuration-management tool you use. This could be a company decision due to budget or security.

Basic usage of Vagrant provisioning

To get started with provisioning our Vagrant machine, let's create a new Vagrantfile. We can do this by running the `vagrant init -m` command.

Within our Vagrantfile, we can define a provisioning block by using the `config.vm.provision` code and pass in a value to declare what type of provisioner we will be using. In the following example, we will be using the shell type:

```
config.vm.provision "shell"
```

Using the shell provisioner, you can then define additional values inline:

```
config.vm.provision "shell", inline "sudo apt-get update -y"
```

Or use a configuration block, where we define our shell value within pipe characters:

```
config.vm.provision "shell" do |shell|
    shell.inline = "sudo apt-get update -y"
  end
```

Both options would, in this example, update the system packages. Using the configuration block method is much easier to read, as each value can have its own line.

Vagrant provisioning commands

Once you've created your provisioner values, it's time to apply those changes to your Vagrant machine. There are a few options:

- When you run the `vagrant up` command for the first time, your machine will read the Vagrantfile and run the provisioner script.
- If you have a machine that has been halted or you want to force a provision, you can run `vagrant up --provision` to enable provisioning.
- You can also use the `--no-provision` flag to disable provisioning.
- Within the provision the config block, you can set a key of `run` and a value of `always`, which will force the provisioner script to run every time a machine is started up. An example of this would be `config.vm.provision "shell", inline: "sudo apt-get update -y", run: "always"`.

The final option will only work if the `--no-provision` flag has not been set.

Vagrant provisioning with a file

The Vagrant file option gives you an easy way to copy a file from your host machine onto the Vagrant machine during the startup process.

This can be a great way of uploading a configuration file that would otherwise need to be created by the software or possibly required before the software can start working. An example of this would be an `.env` file that holds environment variables, such as database-connection details or special keys.

There are two options available – you can copy/upload a single file or an entire directory from your host machine to the guest Vagrant machine.

When using this option, we set the provision option to `file` in our Vagrantfile, for example:

```
config.vm.provision "file"
```

Single file

Uploading a file from the host machine to the guest machine is quick and easy. We just need to set the provision type as `file`, the source as the file on our host, and the destination as:

```
Vagrant.configure("2") do |config|
    config.vm.provision "file", source: "secret.env", destination:
 "secret.env"
  end
```

This will copy our `secret.env` file into the home folder of our Vagrant guest machine.

If that `secret.env` file does not exist, Vagrant will throw an error during the startup process:

```
Bringing machine 'default' up with 'virtualbox' provider...
There are errors in the configuration of this machine. Please fix
the following errors and try again:

File provisioner:
* File upload source file /Users/alexbraunton/Projects/vagrant-provisioning/secret.env
 must exist
```

If the file does exist, then you will see something similar to the following in your console during the startup process:

```
==> default: Running provisioner: file...
```

And after running the `vagrant ssh` command and connecting to the guest machine, we can run the `ls` command to list the files within the directory. We will now see the `secret.env` file:

```
vagrant@ubuntu-xenial:~$ ls
secret.env
```

Directory

Another option is to upload a directory of files and folders from your host machine into your guest machine. This can be useful if you require multiple assets, such as images or configuration files, in a separate and managed way.

It's very similar to the file option when adding this option into our Vagrantfile:

```
Vagrant.configure("2") do |config|
    config.vm.provision "file", source: "secretfolder", destination:
"$HOME/newsecretfolder"
  end
```

We set our source value to be a folder within the current Vagrant directory. You can specify an absolute path if the folder is located elsewhere on your host system.

The destination folder can use the $HOME variable to create the new folder in the home folder of our guest machine. This folder can have the same name or a new name on the guest machine. It depends on your requirements.

We can run the vagrant up --provision command to start up the Vagrant machine. We will see the message again in the output during the process:

```
==> default: Running provisioner: file...
```

Once the machine is up-and-running, we can run the vagrant ssh command machine and run the ls command. We will then see the folder in the home directory. If we run the ls newsecretfolder/ command to view the contents of our new folder, we will see the secret.env file:

```
vagrant@ubuntu-xenial:~$ ls
newsecretfolder
vagrant@ubuntu-xenial:~$ ls newsecretfolder/
secret.env
```

 Please note: When using this option compared to the synced folder featured, any changes made on the host/local machine will not be reflected on the guest machine.

Vagrant Shell provisioner

We've seen how to use a basic shell provisioner, but depending on your setup and required environment, you may have quite a large, complex provisioner script. This script may require arguments or environment variables, or may be linked to an external resource hosted elsewhere.

In this section, we will look at the many options available when using shell as a Vagrant provisioner. This is often used by beginners but can be very powerful and flexible, especially if you do not want to set up configuration-management tools such as Chef and Ansible.

When using the shell provisioner, there are optional configuration settings available:

- **args**: These are arguments that you specify for use by the provisioning script. This can be a string or an array of values.
- **env**: This is a list of key-value pairs (hash) as environment variables to the script.
- **binary**: Vagrant by default replaces Windows line endings with Unix line endings, unless you change this value to true.
- **privileged**: This allows you to change whether the script will be run by a privileged user, such as `sudo`. The default value is true.
- **upload_path**: This is the path on the guest machine that the script will be uploaded to. The SSH user account must have access to write to that folder/file location, otherwise this will fail.
- **keep_color**: Vagrant currently outputs success messages in green and error messages in red. If you change this value to false, this behavior will be stopped.
- **name**: This can be used to identify the provisioner output if there are many different provisioners running in the process.
- **powershell_args**: These are arguments that can be passed to the provisioner if you are using PowerShell on Windows.
- **powershell_elevated_interactive**: This is used when trying to elevate a script in interactive mode on Windows. You must enable auto-login on Windows and the user must be logged in for this to work.
- **md5**: The MD5 value (checksum) is used to verify downloaded shell files.
- **sha1**: The SHA1 value (checksum) is used to verify downloaded shell files.
- **sensitive**: If you specify values in the `env` option, it will mark these as sensitive and not show them in the output.

We'll focus on inline scripts, external scrips, and script arguments.

Inline Scripts

We've briefly touched upon inline scripts, but there are more options available that can be added into the configuration for provisioning.

You can run a script inline using the following syntax:

```
config.vm.provision "shell", inline: "sudo apt-get update -y && echo
updating finished"
```

Or you could create a variable outside the block and use that variable for a cleaner and easier-to-read format:

```
$shellscript = <<-SCRIPT
 sudo apt-get update -y
 echo updating finished
 SCRIPT

config.vm.provision "shell", inline: $shellscript
```

You can experiment with both options and see what works best for you. You may find that, when working on a development team, they already have a syntax you must follow when creating and editing Vagrantfiles.

External scripts

Another option when using shell provisioning is to use external scripts. This can be a good way to keep your script separate, which means it's easier to manage and helps keep your Vagrantfile tidy.

To use an external script, we can use the following syntax:

```
config.vm.provision "shell", path: "[FILELOCATION]"
```

In the preceding example, the "[FILELOCATION]" placeholder could be one of two different options:

- A local script on your machine; an example value would be `script.sh`
- A remote script hosted externally; an example value would be `https://example.com/dev/script.sh`

One benefit of using a remote script is that anyone who is using that Vagrantfile to run a specific machine configuration will always get the most up-to-date version. If you are on a team of developers and a change is made to the provisioner script, all of the other developers just need to run the `vagrant up --provision` command and will then be using the same machine.

Script arguments

Another great feature of shell provisioning is the option of using arguments. These are values that can be passed in as variables and can be easier to manage when data is dynamic.

Script arguments can be passed in as a string or as an array. A string is useful when only one argument is required and an array is useful when multiple arguments are required.

Script argument – string

The following is a syntax example when using a string script argument in your Vagrantfile:

```
config.vm.provision :shell do |shell|
    shell.inline = "echo $1"
    shell.args = "'this is a test'"
end
```

When the *vagrant up* process hits the provisioning stage, we will see an output echoed onto the screen with a value of `this is a test`:

```
==> default: Running provisioner: shell...
    default: Running: inline script
    default: this is a test
```

 Please note: You must remember to properly escape your string. In this case, we are wrapping the string within single quotes. The system would essentially see the 'this is a test' echo, which would not throw any errors.

Script argument – array

Here is the syntax example when using an array script argument in your Vagrantfile:

```
config.vm.provision :shell do |shell|
    shell.inline = "echo $1 $2"
    shell.args = ["this is", "a test"]
  end
```

Similarly to the string argument option, when this provisioner is started within the *vagrant up* process, we will see an output echoed on the screen with a value of this is a test:

```
==> default: Running provisioner: shell...
    default: Running: inline script
    default: this is a test
```

Please note: It's not necessary to quote the individual values in the array. It is still recommended you escape any special characters to minimize any errors.

Summary

In this chapter, we learned about Vagrant provisioning and configuration management. We provisioned a Vagrant machine using the basic usage type, file type, and shell type using inline and external scripts with arguments.

In Chapter 10, *Ansible - Using Ansible to Provision a Vagrant Box*, we will learn more about the Ansible configuration-management tool, and use that to provision a Vagrant machine. We will learn how to use Ansible and Ansible playbooks, including the syntax.

10
Ansible - Using Ansible to Provision a Vagrant Box

In the second part in our provisioning series, we will be learning about Ansible and how to use it to provision a Vagrant machine. The following are the topics we're going to cover in this chapter:

- Understanding Ansible
- Installing Ansible on macOS
- Provisioning Vagrant using Ansible on the host machine
- Provisioning Vagrant using Ansible on the guest machine
- Ansible Playbooks

By the end of this chapter, you will feel confident using Ansible to provision Vagrant machines. You will have a good understanding of how Ansible works and will have links to Vagrant, and will be able to use Ansible on both the host machine and Vagrant machine by using Playbooks to configure exactly what you need.

Understanding Ansible

Ansible is an open source piece of software used to make *IT automation simple* and offers *automation for everyone*. Ansible is a tool used for configuration management, software provisioning, and application deployment. It's a powerful tool that offers many features. These features include the following:

- It can run locally on the host or guest machine
- It has an extensive plugin ecosystem
- It can orchestrate infrastructure using many cloud providers
- It can be installed on many different operating systems
- It has simple inventory management

- It has simple and powerful automation with Playbooks
- Well-written and extensive documentation

Ansible offers a minimal approach to provisioning your software with an easy to learn syntax and is built to be reliable and secure. We'll learn more about Ansible as we work through this chapter by installing it, creating and testing Playbooks, and provisioning a Vagrant machine.

Some more interesting facts about Ansible are that it is part of Red Hat, it is written in Python and PowerShell, its first release was in February 2012, and there is a web-based interface called Ansible Tower that can be used to make managing Ansible even easier.

Installing Ansible

In this first part, we will learn how to install Ansible on our host machine, which in this instance is the macOS. Later in this chapter, we will learn how to install Ansible on Ubuntu, which will be running inside our guest Vagrant machine.

Installing Ansible on macOS High Sierra (version 10.13)

Before we can start provisioning our Vagrant machine using Ansible, we first need to install it on our host machine. We won't look at any advanced installations – just the basics to get Ansible up and running on our machine. If you are using another operating system, then please feel free to use the excellent Ansible docs available at `https://docs.ansible.com/`:

1. We first need to visit the **Installation Guide** page at `https://docs.ansible.com/ansible/latest/installation_guide/intro_installation.html`.
2. There is a list of supported operating systems, but we need to click on the **Latest Releases on macOS** section.
3. Here, we will see that the preferred option is to install Ansible via `pip`.
4. You can check to see whether you have pip installed by running `pip -v`:

```
[vagrant-ansible] pip -v
zsh: command not found: pip
```

5. If you do not have it installed, then you can run the `sudo easy_install pip` command:

```
[vagrant-ansible] sudo easy_install pip
Password:
Searching for pip
Reading https://pypi.python.org/simple/pip/
Best match: pip 18.0
```

You'll need to enter your system password as the command requires `sudo`.

6. You can now install Ansible by running the `sudo pip install ansible` command:

```
[vagrant-ansible] sudo pip install ansible
Password:
```

Again, you will need to enter your system password as the command requires `sudo`.

7. Finally, we can check that Ansible has been successfully installed by running the `ansible --version` command:

```
[vagrant-ansible] ansible --version
ansible 2.6.3
```

You can see that I have the latest version installed: 2.6.3.

Congratulations – you have successfully installed Ansible! We can now start to configure and provision our Vagrant machine.

Provisioning Vagrant using Ansible

In this section, we will look at two different ways of provisioning Vagrant with Ansible. The first will involve running Ansible on our host (macOS) machine and the second will involve running Ansible on our guest (Ubuntu) machine running inside Vagrant.

 Please Note: We will be using the ubuntu/xenial64 box and the version number is `virtualbox, 20180510.0.0`.

Provisioning Vagrant using Ansible on the host machine

Let's set up a basic Vagrant environment and provision it using Ansible from our host machine. We'll learn how to configure Ansible in the Vagrantfile and install software into our Vagrant guest machine running Ubuntu:

1. Let's create a new Vagrantfile in a new directory to start afresh. We can run the `vagrant init -m` command to do this.

2. In our Vagrant file, we'll set the box as Ubuntu by adding in the `config.vm.box = "ubuntu/xenial64"` line and also the networking line:

   ```
   config.vm.network "private_network", ip: "10.10.10.10"
   ```

3. We can now create a `provision` block:

   ```
   config.vm.provision "shell", inline: "sudo apt-get update;
   sudo ln -sf /usr/bin/python3 /usr/bin/python"
     config.vm.provision "ansible" do |ans|    ans.playbook =
   "vagrant_playbook.yml"
     end
   ```

4. Save the Vagrant file and exit your text editor.

If you now run the `vagrant up --provision` command, you will see an error during the final provisioning stage:

```
==> default: Running provisioner: ansible_local...
`playbook` does not exist on the guest: /vagrant/vagrant_playbook.yml
```

This is because Ansible and Vagrant cannot find the playbook `vagrant_playbook.yml`. In the same directory as your Vagrantfile, we will now create our playbook file.

Add in the following code (we'll go through this later so that you know exactly what it does):

```
---
-
  hosts: all
  sudo: true
  tasks:
    -
      apt: "name=nginx state=latest"
      name: "ensure nginx is at the latest version"
```

```
-
name: "start nginx"
service:
 name: nginx
 state: started
```

 Please note: The Playbook file is very strict with regards to its formatting and syntax. You may only use spaces and not tabs in the YAML file. If you have any issues, try removing all spaces and adding natural indent spaces (1 space for top level, 2 spaces for child, and so on). You can use a YAML code/syntax validator tool online (This is the website/tool that I used: http://www.yamllint.com).
This markup will install the latest version of Nginx onto the Vagrant machine. It will then start the Nginx service so that it will be up and running, ready to use. You may need to run the vagrant destroy -f command first if you already have a machine running.

Run the vagrant up --provision command to start the startup process and get Ansible running. You'll see a lot of new coloured output at the provisioning stage, and this will be Ansible installing and configuring Nginx.

The provisioner will start running ansible_local as we specified in the Vagrantfile:

```
==> default: Running provisioner: ansible_local...
    default: Installing Ansible...
```

It will then run the ansible-playbook handler:

```
    default: Running ansible-playbook...
```

Finally, you will see an overview of what Ansible has done (or sometimes not done, which results in a red failure). We can see here that the green ok=3 value means that 3 items have been run successfully, and the yellow changed=1 value means that one item has been changed successfully:

```
PLAY [all] ***********************************************************************

TASK [Gathering Facts] **********************************************************
ok: [default]

TASK [ensure nginx is at the latest version] ***********************************
changed: [default]

TASK [start nginx] *************************************************************
ok: [default]

PLAY RECAP *********************************************************************
default                    : ok=3    changed=1    unreachable=0    failed=0
```

We should now be able to access our Vagrant machine using the IP address of 10.10.10.10 as we set the networking config in the Vagrantfile.

Open up your browser to that IP address and you should see the default Nginx welcome screen:

Congratulations! You have successfully installed Nginx using Ansible to provision Vagrant from your host machine. We covered quite a lot here, but in the next section we will learn more about playbooks.

Provisioning Vagrant using Ansible on the guest machine

Now that we've successfully provisioned our Vagrant machine and installed the Nginx service using the host method, we can learn how to provision Vagrant using Ansible on the guest (Vagrant) machine.

This method is much simpler as it allows everything to be done within the guest machine. You do not require any additional software on your host machine. Vagrant will intelligently try and install Ansible on the guest machine if it cannot be found or accessed.

The following steps are similar to the previous steps, but we'll be adding some additional configuration into our Vagrantfile:

1. Run the `vagrant init -m` command to create a new Vagrantfile (you may need to clear our the current directory or use a new, empty directory if you have followed the previous steps).
2. In our Vagrant file, we'll set the box to be Ubuntu by adding in the `config.vm.box = "ubuntu/xenial64"` line and also the networking line:

   ```
   config.vm.network "private_network", ip: "10.10.10.10"
   ```

3. We can now create a `provision` block:

   ```
   config.vm.provision "ansible_local" do |ans|
           ans.playbook = "vagrant_playbook.yml"
           ans.install = true
           ans.install_mode = "pip"
   end
   ```

4. Save the Vagrantfile and run the `vagrant up --provision` command to get the Vagrant machine up and running.

We'll see a similar process here until Vagrant gets to the provisioning stage. Our guest machine does not have Ansible installed, so it will start to install it. We can see the `ansible_local` provisioner being used here:

```
==> default: Running provisioner: ansible_local...
    default: Installing Ansible...
```

Since we stated that the install mode would be `pip` in our Vagrantfile, the pip package manager will now be installed onto our guest machine:

```
    default: Installing pip... (for Ansible installation)
Vagrant has automatically selected the compatibility mode '2.0'
according to the Ansible version installed (2.6.3).

Alternatively, the compatibility mode can be specified in your Vagrantfile:
https://www.vagrantup.com/docs/provisioning/ansible_common.html#compatibility_mode
```

The Vagrant provisioner will now find and run the Ansible Playbook:

```
    default: Running ansible-playbook...
```

Ansible will now run within the guest machine to install the contents of the Playbook. We can see in the following screenshot that Nginx was installed and started successfully, and that we had no failed elements:

```
PLAY [all] *********************************************************************

TASK [Gathering Facts] ********************************************************
ok: [default]

TASK [ensure nginx is at the latest version] ********************************
changed: [default]

TASK [start nginx] ***********************************************************
ok: [default]

PLAY RECAP ******************************************************************
default                    : ok=3    changed=1    unreachable=0    failed=0
```

We can now visit `10.10.10.10` in our web browser and see the Nginx default page. This will confirm that Nginx has been installed successfully and that the service is running:

Let's now SSH into the Vagrant guest machine by running the `vagrant ssh` command. Once connected, we can run the `ansible --version` command to confirm that Ansible has been installed on our guest system:

```
vagrant@ubuntu-xenial:~$ ansible --version
ansible 2.6.3
```

We can see that the Ansible version that has been installed is 2.6.3. Within our Vagrantfile, we have used some additional Ansible values, which we will learn more about in the next section.

Additional Ansible options

Vagrant supports additional options when using Ansible and Ansible local as a provisioner. These options allow you to add extra functionality and customization to the provisioning process.

Provisioner – Ansible

In this section, we'll look at what additional options can be used with the Ansible provisioner:

- `ask_become_pass`: When set to true (boolean), it will prompt for a password when using the become `sudo` option in Ansible.
- `ask_sudo_pass`: This is essentially ask_become_pass, but will be phased out in future versions of Vagrant. It's used for backward compatibility.
- `ask_vault_pass` : When set to true (boolean), it will force Ansible to prompt for a vault password. Ansible Vault is used to keep sensitive data and passwords encrypted so that you don't have to worry about them being visible in plain text in a Playbook.
- `force_remote_user`: This will require Vagrant to set the `ansible_ssh_user` in the inventory. Ansible will use the `config.ssh.username` value from the Vagrantfile instead of using the `remote_user` parameters in the Ansible Playbook.
- `host_key_checking`: This option will require Ansible to enable SSH host key checking.
- `raw_ssh_args`: This option can be used in order to apply a list of OpenSSH client options. The value is typically an array of strings.

 Please note: It's worth checking out the official Vagrant and Ansible documentation for more in-depth explanations of these options and to find out whether there is anything that you may require but are not quite sure of the name or how it's applied.

Provisioner – Ansible local

In this section, we'll look at what additional options can be used with the Ansible local Provisioner:

- `install`: This option is enabled by default and will attempt to install Ansible on the guest system if it cannot be found/run.
- `install_mode`: This option allows you to choose how Ansible is to be installed on the guest system. You can choose default, `pip`, or `pip_args_only`. The default option will attempt to use the guest operating system's package manager. The pip option will use the Python package manager. The `pip_args_only` option works similarly to the pip option, but does not allow Vagrant to automatically set pip options.

- `pip_args`: This option is used when the `install_mode` is set to use pip. It allows you to pass pip arguments into the command line.
- `provisioning_path`: This is a path to the directory where Ansible files are stored. Commands such as `ansible-playbook` are run from this location.
- `tmp_path`: This is an absolute path on the guest machine where files can be stored temporarily by the Ansible local provisioner.

 Please note: It's worth checking out the official Vagrant and Ansible documentation for more in-depth explanations for these options and to find out whether there is anything that you may require but are not quite sure of the name or how it's applied.

Ansible Playbooks

An Ansible Playbook is a configuration file used by Ansible. You can think of it as a Vagrantfile for Vagrant. It uses the YAML (Yet Another Markup Language) markup language as the syntax and is easily readable:

```
---
- hosts: all
    sudo: yes
    tasks:
        - name: ensure nginx is at the latest version
            apt: name=nginx state=latest
        - name: start nginx
            service:
                name: nginx
                state: started
```

Let's look at the example playbook we created in the previous section, shown here in the above code block, and dissect it to get a better understanding of what it all means:

- The first line is always three dashes to signify the beginning of the file.
- We must then define which hosts this applies to. These can often be defined in the Ansible inventory file by setting a value such as [db] and supplying an IP address for that node.
- We then set the `sudo` value to `yes` as we require sudo/root privileges to install Nginx on the Vagrant guest machine.
- We then move into the tasks section, which is what we want Ansible to do – the provisioning stage. We'll separate each task with a name section. This describes what we want the task to do, for example, `start nginx`.

- Within a task, we can define the actions. In our first one called `apt`, we are calling the package manager (apt-get) to install the latest version of the Nginx package.
- We then move to our final task which makes sure the Nginx service has been started.

I hope you can see from this example that Ansible Playbooks are very easy to read and work down in a logical flow. You'll come across much more complex Playbooks and some similar ones compared to this example, but always follow the indentation within each block to get a better understanding of what each section does.

Summary

In this chapter, we learned how to provision Vagrant using Ansible on the host and guest machine. We've also learned what Ansible is and about Ansible Playbooks. If you use Ansible in your company, then I would recommend trying it with Vagrant to help with your development workflow.

In `Chapter 12`, *Docker - Using Docker with Vagrant*, we will be continuing our series on provisioning by learning about Chef and how to use that configuration management tool to provision Vagrant. We will look at multiple Chef options (solo and client) and learn about Chef cookbooks.

11
Chef - Using Chef to Provision a Vagrant Box

In this chapter, we will continue our series on provisioning Vagrant by using popular DevOps configuration management tools. We will be focusing on Chef and will cover the following topics:

- Understanding Chef
- Chef Cookbook
- Installing Chef on macOS
- Using Chef Solo to provision a Vagrant machine
- Using Chef Client to provision a Vagrant machine

At the end of this chapter, you will have a good understanding of what Chef is and the components that make it work. You will feel confident in using Chef to provision a Vagrant machine, whether that be on the host or on the Vagrant machine itself. You'll understand how to create a Cookbook, which can be a very powerful and flexible tool, so that you can manage your machine's state.

Understanding Chef

Chef is a popular configuration management tool used to configure and maintain servers. It was created by the company named Chef and is written in Ruby and Erlang. It was initially released in January 2009 and is offered in two different versions – free (open source) and paid (enterprise).

Chef supports and integrates with many cloud platforms such as Amazon EC2, OpenStack, Rackspace, and Microsoft Azure. Chef can be run in solo mode (no dependencies) or in client/server mode, where the client communicates with the server and sends information about the node that it's installed on.

Chef uses Cookbooks and recipes as part of its configuration, which we will focus on in the next section.

Chef Cookbook

Chef uses Cookbooks as a key element in its processes and they are used to describe the desired state of your node/server.

A Chef Cookbook is an important part of configuring machines when using Chef. It describes the desired state of the machine. This is similar to using Playbooks in Ansible. The Chef Cookbook contains five key elements, which all have their own part to play:

- Recipes
- Templates
- Attribute values
- Extensions
- File distributors

These elements are often pieces of metadata that work together to create an overview of the machine. Let's dive deeper into these five elements to learn more about them.

 When speaking about a node, we are referring to a machine – whether physical or virtual. The node could be a computer, server, network device, or another machine.

Recipes

A recipe is a key part of the Cookbook. It's used to detail what exactly should happen with a node. It's similar to a Vagrantfile when setting the state for a Vagrant virtual machine.

The recipe is written in Ruby and must be added onto the node's run list, which will then allow the node to run that recipe. A Cookbook can use one or more recipes or rely on outside recipes, too.

A recipe's main aim is to manage resources. A resource could be a software package, service, users, groups, files, directories, cron jobs, and more.

Templates

Templates are a specific type of file that includes embedded Ruby. These files use the .erb extension and can be used to create dynamic configuration files.

These files can access attribute values (which you will learn about in the next section). This is like using variables in the files and not having to hard-code the settings. You could have multiple templates referencing the same attribute and, when one changes, it will change the value in all of the template files.

Attribute values

Attribute values in Chef are essentially settings. They are often displayed as key value pairs. These settings can be used inside the Cookbook.

Attributes are set in the attributes subdirectory of the Cookbook and can then be referenced in other parts of the Cookbook. Attributes can be set at the top (Cookbook) level but can also be overwritten at the node level by any node-specific settings/attributes.

Extensions

These are simply extensions to Chef such as libraries and custom resources. These can also be referred to as *tools*, which you can learn more about in the *Chef Supermarket* section.

File distributors

Static files are used to contain simple configurations. They are placed within the file's subdirectory and are often moved onto the node by a recipe. These files are likely to not be changed and can be thought of as simple, non-dynamic templates.

Chef Supermarket

If you are looking for a specific Cookbook/piece of software, then you can use the Chef Supermarket. You can think of the Chef Supermarket like HashiCorp's Vagrant Cloud. It hosts Cookbooks for you to view and download. The Supermarket is easy to use and offers a simple, fast user interface. Their main feature is the easy-to-use search facility.

Search

If you are looking for a specific Cookbook or just want to see what's available, then you can use the powerful search function. It offers a full text search and a filter to help narrow down the results. You can use the search by visiting the Chef Supermarket home page via the following link: `https://supermarket.chef.io/`:

In the preceding screenshot, you can see the `Search` feature. You can search for specific software packages such as nginx, or something more general to see what is available, such as `web server`.

There are two options when narrowing down your search. The first option is that you can use the **Advanced Options** search option, which can be found underneath the search bar, to the right:

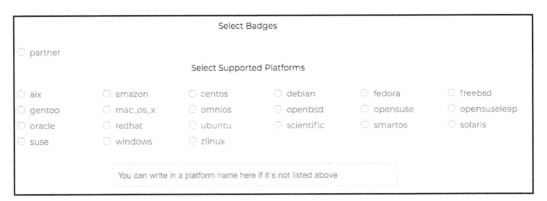

In the preceding screenshot, you see the **Advanced Options** expanded menu, which allows you to filter the search by **Badges** and/or **Selected Supported Platforms**. You can also use the text search bar at the bottom to search for a specific platform if it's not available in the list.

There is currently only one **Badge** option available, which is **partner**. This option searches for Chef partner Cookbooks, which are Cookbooks that have been hand-picked by the Chef engineering team or created by them. We'll look at the other filter option here:

To the left of the search bar, you can select the type you wish to search. There are currently two options – **Cookbooks** and **Tools**. The default is Cookbooks, and this will search through the available Cookbooks. The Tools option will search through the Chef tools that are available. Tools are pieces of software that can be used alongside Chef – these are not plugins as such, but add-ons:

In the preceding screenshot, we are searching for `nginx`, which is the web server. You can see that it has found 43 Cookbooks and you have the option to sort by **Most Followed** and **Recently Updated**. You will see some important information such as the Cookbook version, last update date/time, supported platform, code to install, and follower count.

You can click on the Cookbook name (in this case, `nginx`) to get more information about the Cookbook:

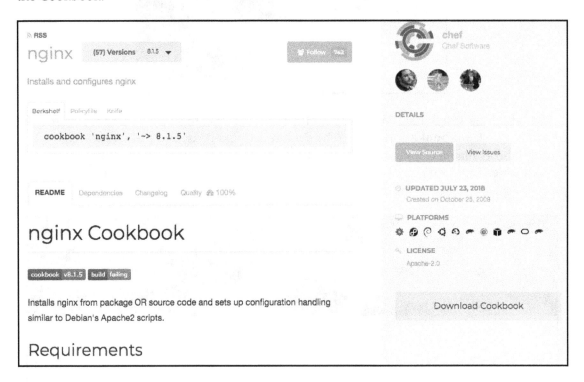

In the preceding screenshot, you can see the Cookbook page. It includes more information, which includes the Cookbook creator/maintainer(s) and gives a detailed readme file. There are other bits of information such as dependencies, change log, installation instructions/options, and more.

Provisioning Vagrant with Chef

There are four different ways to use Chef to provision a Vagrant machine that Vagrant supports. This means that Chef has the most options in Vagrant when it comes to provisioning. The four options are as follows:

- Chef Solo
- Chef Zero
- Chef Client
- Chef Apply

In this chapter, we will be focusing on Chef Solo and Chef Client. This will give you a good mixture of provisioning on the host machine and the Vagrant machine.

Installing Chef on macOS

Before we can begin using Chef, we will first need to install it. We'll learn how to install Chef on the macOS operating system (the High Sierra 10.13 version).

We'll be installing the Chef DK (development kit), which includes all of the dependencies, utilities, and the main Chef software. The list of installed software includes the following:

- Chef client
- OpenSSL
- Embedded Ruby
- RubyGems
- Command-line utilites
- Key value stores
- Parsers
- Utilities
- Libraries
- Community tools such as Kitchen and ChefSpec

 Please Note: The Apple XCode software package is required before you are able to install Chef.

Let's now install and test Chef on our system:

1. Go to the Chef DK downloads page (the following is a link to the macOS section: `https://downloads.chef.io/chefdk#mac_os_x`).

2. Find the version you are currently running on your system and click the orange **Download** button, as follows:

3. Run the `.dmg` file installer. You'll need to first run the installer file. Click on the `.pkg` file to run it.

4. The installer will run and you'll be prompted to move through the six steps. Please follow these. We will not be changing any values during this installation:

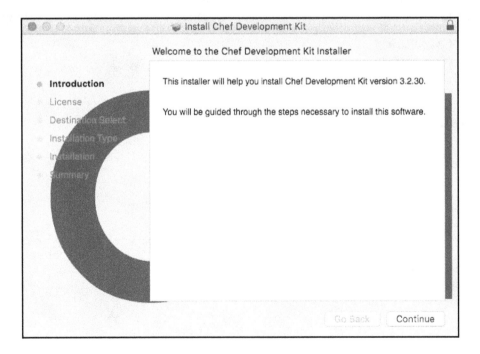

5. Once complete, you should see the *green tick* success screen. Close this window by clicking on the **Close** button. This will then allow you to move the installer package into the trash.

6. To confirm that Chef has been installed, open a terminal window and run the `chef -v` command, which should list the Chef version and other dependencies:

```
[vagrant-chef] chef -v
Chef Development Kit Version: 3.2.30
chef-client version: 14.4.56
delivery version: master (6862f27aba89109a9630f0b6c6798efec56b4efe)
berks version: 7.0.6
kitchen version: 1.23.2
inspec version: 2.2.70
```

As you can see, there are many pieces of software running with Chef. There is the DK version, the chef-client version, the kitchen version, and more. Knowing these versions can come in handy if you have to debug any issues (with specific pieces of software) in the future.

Congratulations! You now have Chef installed on your system. Let's now look at provisioning a Vagrant machine using Chef.

Using Chef Solo to provision a Vagrant machine

Similar to previous chapters, we will stick with our example of installing the nginx web server on our Vagrant machine. Although this is a simple example, it does allow us to use a popular piece of software and configure networking, and is a simple way of seeing if it was a success.

Using Chef Solo as a provisioner for Vagrant is a quick and easy way to get started with Chef. It has no dependencies (apart from Chef itself) and can be used by beginners or advanced users.

We'll first need to create our Vagrantfile by running the `vagrant init -m` command.

Inside our Vagrantfile, let's specify the box and networking for the IP address. Let's also specify our provisioner and configure chef-solo while we are inside the Vagrantfile. Your finished file should look like the following:

```
Vagrant.configure("2") do |config|
    config.vm.box = "ubuntu/xenial64"
    config.vm.network "private_network", ip: "10.10.10.10"
    config.vm.provision "chef_solo" do |ch|
        ch.add_recipe "nginx"
    end
end
```

We have set `config.vm.provision` to `chef_solo` and within this block we are setting the `add_recipe` value to `nginx`. This means that we are telling Vagrant to specifically use the `nginx` recipe. Vagrant will look inside the `cookbooks` folder, which is in the root of our project (where the Vagrantfile is).

Before we can run the Vagrant machine, we need to do some Chef groundwork. Here, we are going to create the `nginx` recipe. We'll use the official nginx Cookbook from the Chef Supermarket, which can be found via the following link: `https://supermarket.chef.io/cookbooks/nginx`.

Be default, Vagrant will look for a `cookbooks` directory inside the project root (where the Vagrantfile is located). Let's first create this folder on our host by running the `mkdir cookbooks` command. Let's now move into this directory by running the `cd cookbooks` command in our terminal.

To satisfy the supermarket command, we'll need a local git repository. Let's create a basic repository and commit to get started. Run the following commands to achieve the minimum requirements:

- `git init`
- `touch null`
- `git add -A`
- `git commit -m 'null'`

Let's install this recipe using the `knife` command-line utility that we installed earlier. On the supermarket page, we can see two commands. Let's run the `install` command:

```
knife supermarket install nginx --cookbook-path .
```

This should install the `nginx` Cookbook (folder) into your Cookbooks `directory`. We can confirm this by running the `ls` and `ls cookbooks` commands inside our project directory:

```
[vagrant-chef] ls
Vagrantfile cookbooks
[vagrant-chef] ls cookbooks
nginx
```

Let's now run the `vagrant up --provision` command (back in the root directory, not in the Cookbooks directory) to start and provision the Vagrant machine. During the provision stage, you should see the `Running chef-solo...` message, which means that the provisioner has started. You will now see lots of green output, which is Chef starting up, installing the dependencies, and running the nginx Cookbook. The `nginx` service (once installed) should start running automatically:

```
==> default: Running provisioner: chef_solo...
    default: Installing Chef (latest)...
==> default: Generating chef JSON and uploading...
==> default: Running chef-solo...
==> default: [2018-09-10T22:04:23+00:00] INFO: Started chef-zero at chefzero://localho
st:1 with repository at /tmp/vagrant-chef/67a6d709eb65f4596491f85f27e65cc3, /tmp/vagra
nt-chef
==> default:    One version per cookbook
==> default: Starting Chef Client, version 14.4.56
==> default: [2018-09-10T22:04:23+00:00] INFO: *** Chef 14.4.56 ***
```

If you now visit `http://10.10.10.10` in your browser, you should see nginx's default page:

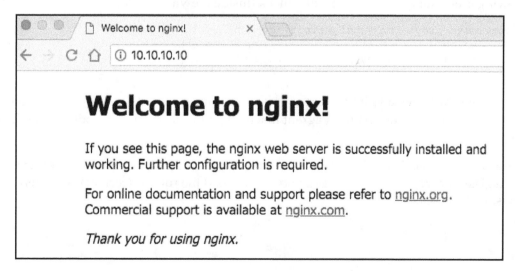

Congratulations! You have successfully installed nginx onto a Vagrant machine using the Chef Solo provisioner.

 This was a simple example of using Chef Solo with Vagrant. Please do not be fooled into thinking this technique isn't powerful. You can experiment with far more complicated Cookbooks.

Using Chef Client to provision a Vagrant machine

Although the *Chef Client* provisioner can be seen as the advanced option, it's actually much simpler and quicker to set up than the *Chef Solo* provisioner, which we looked at in the previous section.

The reason why the Chef Client provisioner is simpler and quicker is that it is just a client. It's essentially a zombie which does not think for itself. It uses a Chef Server to get its commands and Cookbook files. When managing a large infrastructure, using this Client-to-Server method can be a much easier way than having to manage multiple nodes separately.

We won't cover how to set up a Chef Server in this book, as it's beyond its scope, but you can learn more from the official Chef documentation website here: `https://docs.chef.io/install_server.html`.

There isn't much to cover in this section, since the Chef Server handles the main bulk of the work, but there are some configuration settings we can add in the Vagrantfile. The following is an example of the provision block (inside the Vagrantfile):

```
config.vm.provision "chef_client" do |ch|
    ch.chef_server_url = "https://www.examplechefserver.com"
    ch.validation_key_path = "cert.pem"
end
```

We are using two new keys here: `chef_server_url` and `validation_key_path` – both of which are required to connect the Vagrant machine (in this instance, the node) to the Chef Server.

We must set the Chef Server's URL and the path to the validation key (a `.pem` file). This will then register the Vagrant machine as a node, download the run list (recipes), and then provision the machine.

Summary

In this chapter, we learned about provisioning a Vagrant machine with Chef. We did this by using Chef Cookbooks to create a recipe which controls which software to install onto the Vagrant machine using either Chef Solo or Chef Client.

In `Chapter 12`, *Docker - Using Docker with Vagrant*, we will learn how to use Docker to provision a Vagrant machine. We will learn about Docker images, containers, and the Docker hub. We will then explore the multiple Docker options that are available when provisioning a Vagrant machine.

12
Docker - Using Docker with Vagrant

In this chapter, we will learn how to provision a Vagrant machine using Docker. This is not to be confused with the Docker provider, which is used to power and manage Vagrant machines. We currently use the VirtualBox provider for this.

We'll dive deep into the Docker provisioner and see what is available within Vagrant when using Docker. Specifically, you'll learn about the following topics:

- Understanding Docker
- Key components of Docker (Docker Hub, containers, and images)
- How to find and pull in an image from the Docker Hub
- Basic usage such as running a container
- The Docker-specific configuration within Vagrant

By the end of this chapter, you should have a good understanding of what Docker is and how it can be used as a provisioner with Vagrant.

Understanding Docker

You've probably heard of Docker—even if you've never used it. It's incredibly popular at the moment and is being used/adopted by many companies. Docker is a tool that allows you to manage your applications using a type of virtualization known as containerization. Applications are bundled into containers and can be hosted in the cloud or using your own hardware. There are various tools used to manage Docker containers such as Docker Swarm and Kubernetes.

Docker was released in March 2015 by Solomon Hykes. Its current release is 18.06.1 and it is written using the Go programming language. It can run on Windows, Linux, and macOS.

Docker belongs to the same virtualization family as Vagrant, VMWare, and VirtualBox. It also belongs to the same provisioning and infrastructure family as Chef, Puppet, and Ansible.

There are many benefits from using Docker over other virtualization software. It's mainly a lightweight and faster alternative because it runs in a different way from traditional virtual machines.

Docker uses the Docker Engine, which sits on top of the operating system and shares components such as the host OS kernel, libraries, and binaries (which are read-only). This means that containers can be started fast and are small in size. Traditional virtualization uses a hypervisor that sits on top of the operating system; this in turn creates whole new OSes with their own libraries and binaries. The advantage of this is that you can package up a whole system, but this also means that it can be slow and large in terms of file size. Of course, both alternatives have their benefits, depending on your requirements.

Key components of Docker

When talking about Docker, there are a few main components that you will hear mentioned. Let's learn more about each one in the following subsections.

Containers

A container is portable, lightweight, and a package of software that has everything needed to run an application. A container runs on the Docker Engine and shares the host operating system's kernel between other containers. A container is basically a running instance of a Docker image.

Images

A Docker image is a file that is made up of different layers. These layers include tools, dependencies, and system libraries, which are then used to create a container. There are often base images that available to use, such as the Ubuntu one. You can use multiple images to separate your application, for example, having an image for your web server (Nginx) and another for your database (MySQL).

Registry

Docker offers a hosted registry called Docker Hub. It allows you to browse, pull, and store Docker images. You can think of it like the Vagrant Cloud, which offers hosting for Vagrant boxes along with other features such as downloading and searching boxes. We'll learn more about Docker Hub in the following section.

Service

In Docker, services can be thought of as groupings of specific application logic. Services are often containers in production and help manage your Docker setup. There are specific tools that are used to manage and orchestrate Docker, such as Docker Swarm and Kubernetes. When you reach a certain scale or require more control, then these tools are useful.

Using the Docker Hub to find Docker images

Docker Hub is Docker's online, hosted registry for Docker images. It allows you to search, pull, and store images in the cloud. It's similar to Hashicorp's Vagrant Cloud or the Chef Supermarket. You can access the Hub by visiting its website at `https://hub.docker.com/`.

Docker Hub also offers some really interesting features, including the following:

- Build and test your images
- It links to Docker Cloud, which allows you to deploy your images to your hosts
- Workflow/pipeline automation
- A centralized resource for container discovery
- User accounts
- Public and private registries

Let's take a look at the Docker Hub and use the search facility to find an image:

1. Visit the website at `https://hub.docker.com/`.
2. Click on the **Explore** link in the top right menu.
3. You'll now see the **Explore** screen, which lists the top official repositories.

4. In the top left, there is a search bar. Let's search for `memcached` and view the results:

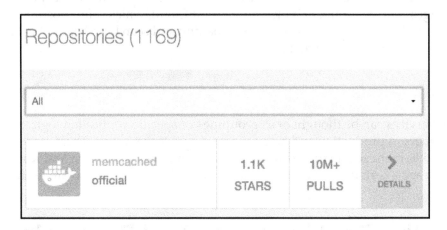

We can see that it found **1169** repositories, and the top one is the official repository, with over 1 thousand stars and 10 million pulls.

5. You can now filter the search results by clicking on the drop-down that has the **All** value selected:

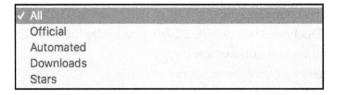

6. Let's click the top result and learn more about the official **memcached** repository:

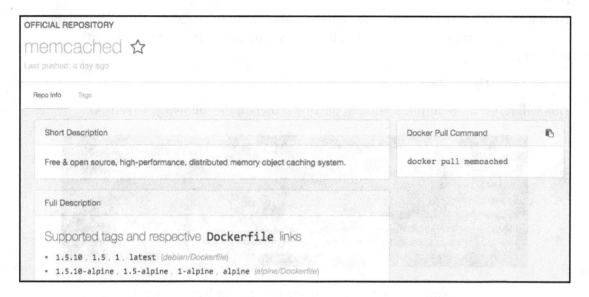

Here, you can see lots of information related to this image. There is a **Short Description** and a **Full Description**. The **Full Description** has information regarding how to use the image, licensing, and different versions that are available. To the right, you can see the **Docker Pull Command**, which is `docker pull memcached`. This is the command that you can run to pull an image down so that you can use it with your installation of Docker.

Basic usage – running a container

We won't delve too deeply into running Docker as a separate tool. Our focus in this chapter is on using Docker to provision a Vagrant machine, which it does inside Vagrant during the boot up process. We will learn a few basic Docker commands—mainly those that are used during provisioning—to give you a better understanding of what is happening.

If you are unsure of what specific command you need or would like to learn more, then you can run the `docker` command, which will list all available commands. This will show you the usage, command options, management commands, and general commands.

Please note: you must have Docker installed to run these commands, or you will get an error.

pull

To pull an image down from the Docker Hub, you can use the `docker pull` command. An example of this command would be pulling down the `nginx` image by running the following:

```
docker pull nginx
```

This will result in an output similar to the one shown in the following screenshot:

```
[vagrant-docker] docker pull nginx
Using default tag: latest
latest: Pulling from library/nginx
802b00ed6f79: Pull complete
e9d0e0ea682b: Pull complete
d8b7092b9221: Pull complete
Digest: sha256:24a0c4b4a4c0eb97a1aabb8e29f18e917d05abfe1b7a7c07857230879ce7d3d3
Status: Downloaded newer image for nginx:latest
```

We can then check to make sure that this image is available by running the `docker images` command:

```
[vagrant-docker] docker images
REPOSITORY          TAG          IMAGE ID          CREATED          SIZE
nginx               latest       06144b287844      9 days ago       109MB
```

run

To start a new container, you can use the `docker run` command. An example of this command would be running the `nginx` image:

```
docker run nginx
```

This will start the Nginx container. You won't see anything on the screen apart from the command:

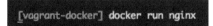

```
[vagrant-docker] docker run nginx
```

If you open another tab in your Terminal and run the `docker ps -a` command, you will see any active running containers. In the following screenshot, you'll see our Docker container:

stop

To stop a Docker container, you can use the `docker stop` command. An example of this command would be running the following:

```
docker stop sleepy_dijkstra
```

We have passed in the `sleepy_dijkstra` container name from the preceding example. We have found the image name by running `docker ps -a`. If we now run the `docker ps -a` command, we'll see that the status is `Exited (0) 3 seconds ago`. In the following screenshot, you'll be able to see the two commands and their output:

start

This command is used to start a previously stopped Docker container. To do this, you can use the `docker start` command. An example of this command would be running the following:

```
docker start sleepy_dijkstra
```

We have passed in the `sleepy_dijkstra` container name from the preceding example. We have found the image name by running `docker ps -a`. If we now run the `docker ps -a` command, we'll see that the status is `Up 4 seconds`. In the following screenshot, you'll be able to see the two commands and their output:

```
[vagrant-docker] docker start sleepy_dijkstra
sleepy_dijkstra
[vagrant-docker] docker ps -a
CONTAINER ID    IMAGE       COMMAND                CREATED          STATUS          PORTS       NAMES
3a4ba61f6312    nginx       "nginx -g 'daemon of…"  10 minutes ago   Up 4 seconds    80/tcp      sleepy_dijkstra
```

search

You can search the Docker Hub from the command line using the `docker search` command. An example of this command would be searching for `ubuntu` by using the following command:

```
docker search ubuntu
```

This will result in an output similar to the one shown in the following screenshot:

```
[vagrant-docker] docker search ubuntu
NAME                                          DESCRIPTION                                      STARS    OFFICIAL
ubuntu                                        Ubuntu is a Debian-based Linux operating sys…    8385     [OK]
doromu/ubuntu-desktop-lxde-vnc                Ubuntu with openssh-server and NoVNC             218
rastasheep/ubuntu-sshd                        Dockerized SSH service, built on top of offi…   170
consol/ubuntu-xfce-vnc                        Ubuntu container with "headless" VNC session…   129
ansible/ubuntu14.04-ansible                   Ubuntu 14.04 LTS with ansible                    95
ubuntu-upstart                                Upstart is an event-based replacement for th…    89       [OK]
neurodebian                                   NeuroDebian provides neuroscience research s…    54       [OK]
1and1internet/ubuntu-16-nginx-php-phpmyadmin-mysql-5    ubuntu-16-nginx-php-phpmyadmin-mysql-5    44
ubuntu-debootstrap                            debootstrap --variant=minbase --components=m…    39       [OK]
```

Similar to searching on the Docker Hub website, you will be presented with a list of search results. These are ordered by the highest, starting at the top. You'll see the image name, description, star count, and whether it's official. You can then pull an image down using the `docker pull [imagename]` command.

Using Docker to provision a Vagrant machine

Now that we've learned a bit about Docker, we can get to the fun part! In this section, we will go through an example of using Docker to provision a Vagrant machine. One thing to note is that Vagrant will attempt to install Docker so that you don't have to. Interestingly, Docker is run within the Vagrant machine, not on your host machine. You'll see this as you will be able to SSH into the Vagrant machine and run Docker commands.

Let's get started and provision our Vagrant machine using Docker:

1. To begin, run the `vagrant init -m` command to create a minimal Vagrantfile.
2. In our Vagrantfile, let's add in a provision block:

```
Vagrant.configure("2") do |config|
    config.vm.box = "ubuntu/xenial64"
    config.vm.network "forwarded_port", guest: 80, host: 8081
    config.vm.provision "docker" do |doc|
        doc.run "nginx", args: "-p 80:80"
    end
end
```

We've set a few default values to get started. We are using the `"ubuntu/xenial64"` box and we specify that the networking should use a port forwarder from the host (`8081`) to the guest (`80`).

In the provision block, we are setting `docker` to be our provisioner. We are using the `run` option and passing in the `"nginx"` image. Alongside the run option, we are passing in the `args` option and setting the value to `"-p 80:80"`, which tells Docker to publish the container's port to the host machine. This is why we are setting the port forwarding to the guest `port 80`. Due to this, we can access the Docker container:

3. Now, let's run the `vagrant up` command to get the machine started. During the provisioning stage, you should see something similar to the following screenshot:

```
==> default: Running provisioner: docker...
    default: Installing Docker onto machine...
==> default: Starting Docker containers...
==> default: -- Container: nginx
```

There are a few steps here. First, it runs the `docker` provisioner, and then installs Docker onto the machine. Once installed, it will start the Docker containers (this is what we specified by using the `run` option in the Vagrantfile) and you'll see the container output as `-- Container: nginx`.

4. To test whether everything was successful, we can open a browser and visit the following link: `http://localhost:8081`. This should connect us to the container using Vagrant's port forwarding:

In the preceding screenshot, we can see Nginx's default welcome page. This is great news and means everything is working as it should.

5. We can also SSH into the Vagrant machine and access Docker through the Terminal. Run the `vagrant ssh` command to gain access.

6. Once in the machine, run the `docker ps -a` command to list any actively running containers:

In the preceding screenshot, we can see the `nginx` container running.

Congratulations! You have successfully provisioned a Vagrant machine using Docker. It's a fairly straightforward process, but can be very powerful. If you use Docker for other parts of the application lifestyle, then you can now try using it for development.

Docker-specific configuration in Vagrant

When it comes to the Docker-specific options in the Vagrantfile, there are none that are required. If do not enter any options, then Vagrant will simply attempt to install Docker—unless you already have it installed.

Images

If you want Docker to use specific images, then you can pass in an array of image names. In your Vagrantfile, an example would be as follows:

```
Vagrant.configure("2") do |config|
    config.vm.provision "docker", images: ["nginx"]
  end
```

This would attempt to pull down the `nginx` image. There are other options that can be used to handle images: `build_image` and `pull_images`; we will cover these in the following sections.

build_image

As well as running and pulling down images, you can actually build an image before it is then used as part of provisioning and its process. The build is done on the Vagrant guest machine and must be available for Docker to access. It runs the `docker build` command, so all you have to do is pass in the location of the Dockerfile.

An example of using this in a Vagrantfile would be as follows:

```
Vagrant.configure("2") do |config|
    config.vm.provision "docker" do |dock|
        dock.build_image "/vagrant/provision"
    end
  end
```

Here, we are using the `dock.build_image` key inside the provision block to set the directory (where our Dockerfile is located).

args

With the `build_images` key, there is an additional parameter called `args`. This allows you to pass in arguments that will be run as part of the `docker build` command. The value will be passed as a string.

To add in the `--pull` flag (which always attempts to pull in the latest version of the image) into the build process, the Vagrantfile might look as follows:

```
Vagrant.configure("2") do |config|
    config.vm.provision "docker" do |dock|
        dock.build_image "/vagrant/provision", args: "--pull"
    end
end
```

In order to pass in multiple parameters/flags, just add them into the string. There is no need to use an array.

pull_images

Another way to handle images during provisioning is to use the `pull_images` option in your Vagrantfile. This option will attempt to pull the images from the Docker registry and use those.

An example Vagrantfile would be as follows:

```
Vagrant.configure("2") do |config|
    config.vm.provision "docker" do |dock|
        dock.pull_images "nginx"
        dock.pull_images "mysql"
    end
end
```

This code attempts to pull down the `nginx` and `mysql` images. The `pull_images` option can be used multiple times and will append them, while the `images` option can only be used once.

run

The run option is used in the Vagrantfile to start and run specific Docker containers. This is done during the vagrant up process. It runs the docker run command to achieve this.

Here's how it would be used in a Vagrantfile:

```
Vagrant.configure("2") do |config|
    config.vm.provision "docker" do |dock|
        dock.run "nginx"
    end
  end
```

In the preceding example, we are instructing the Docker provisioner to run the nginx container. You can use the run option multiple times, but if you use the same image, then you must define seperate names/identifiers for them. The following is an example of using the nginx image twice with different names:

```
Vagrant.configure("2") do |config|
    config.vm.provision "docker" do |dock|
        dock.run "load-balancer", image: "nginx"
        dock.run "web-server", image: "nginx"
    end
  end
```

One can be identified as the load balancer and the other as the web server. You can choose the names here, but I find that descriptive ones are usually the best and easiest to understand.

image

This is actually the default value when using the run option, and it's the first parameter you pass, for example, the image name. It can, however, be passed as an option, such as in the preceding example, when you wish to run two of the same images.

An example within the provision block of your Vagrantfile would be as follows:

```
dock.run "lb1", image: "nginx"
```

In the preceding example, we are referencing the run option and also the image option. The image we have chosen is nginx.

cmd

This cmd option allows you to pass in a command that will be run within the container. If this value is omitted, then the container's default value will be used. This could be the cmd value, which is supplied in the Dockerfile.

An example within the provision block of your Vagrantfile would be as follows:

```
dock.run "ubuntu", cmd: "echo $HOME"
```

In the preceding example, we are referencing the run option and the cmd option. The cmd option will simply run that command within the container. It just accesses the $HOME environment variable, which is the user's home path directory.

args

Using the args option allows you to pass in arguments to the docker run command. This is similar to the additional args option that's used in the build_image section. This can be useful if you require something more granular than the general command.

An example within the provision block of your Vagrantfile would be as follows:

```
dock.run "ubuntu", args: "--name ubuntumain"
```

In the preceding example, we are referencing the run command and the args option. The args option will pass in the parameter to the docker run command when necessary. In our example, it is passing the --name flag with a value of ubuntumain. This will be the name of the container.

auto_assign_name

Using the auto_assign_name option allows you to automatically name the Docker containers. It works by essentially passing the --name flag and a value. This is enabled by default, and the value is true. One thing to note is that any slashes in the image name (for example, base/archlinux) will be replaced with dashes so that the image will become base-archlinux. The name is selected by the first argument of the run.

In the following example we are setting the run option value to nginx so that the container will automatically be named to nginx. The only way to override this is to set the auto_assign_name value to false, which we will do:

```
dock.run "nginx", auto_assign_name: false
```

deamonize

This option allows you to deamonize the containers. The default value for this option is true. It passes the −d flag into the `docker run` command. If you do not want to deamonize the containers, then you can set the value to false.

An example within the provision block of your Vagrantfile would be as follows:

```
dock.run "nginx", deamonize: false
```

In the preceding example, we are using the `run` option and the `deamonize` option. The deamonize option is passing the false value to let Docker know that we do not want it to run as a deamon, so the −d flag will not be passed to Docker.

restart

This option allows you to set the restart policy for the container. The default value is `always`, but it also supports `no`, `unless-stopped`, and `on-failure`. This option can be useful if you have a specific requirement and need control over the restart policy for one or more of your containers.

An example within the provision block of your Vagrantfile would be as follows:

```
dock.run "nginx", restart: "no"
```

In the preceding example, we are using the `run` option and the `restart` option. The restart option is passing the `no` value, which tells Docker not to restart when a container exits.

post_install_provisioner

Using the `post_install_provisioner` option offers you an easy way to run a provisioner once the original provisioner has run. This sounds a little confusing, but it essentially allows you to create a new provision block within the Docker one. You could use Docker as your main provisioner and then, inside, use a shell provisioner which runs when the Docker one has finished.

An example Vagrantfile would look like this:

```
Vagrant.configure("2") do |config|
    config.vm.box = "ubuntu/xenial64"
    config.vm.network "forwarded_port", guest: 80, host: 8081
    config.vm.provision "docker" do |dock|
        dock.post_install_provision "shell", inline:"touch
/vagrant/index.html && echo '<h1>Hello World!</h1>' > /vagrant/index.html"
        dock.run "nginx",
            args: "-p 80:80 -v '/vagrant:/usr/share/nginx/html'"
    end
end
```

The preceding code will run the `nginx` Docker image and then use the shell provisioner. The shell provisioner will run a script inside the Vagrant machine that simply changes the content in the default landing page of Nginx.

When you run the preceding example, you should be able to visit `http://localhost:8081` on your host machine (once the provisioning has completed) and see a large `Hello World!` message.

Summary

In this chapter, we have learned about Docker and how it can be used to configure a Vagrant machine. We have also learned how Docker works, how to use Docker Hub, and the various Docker-specific Vagrantfile options that are available. You should now be able to experiment with Docker as a provider.

In Chapter 13, *Puppet – Using Puppet to Provision a Vagrant Box*, you will learn how to use Puppet to provision a Vagrant machine. We'll focus on the two main supported types—Puppet Apply and Puppet Agent.

13
Puppet - Using Puppet to Provision a Vagrant Box

In this chapter, we will continue with provisioning and learn how to provision a Vagrant machine using the Puppet software. In this chapter, you will learn about the following topics:

- Understanding Puppet
- What Puppet apply and Puppet agent are
- What the Puppet manifest is
- How to provision a Vagrant machine with Puppet

At the end of this chapter, you will have a good understanding of how Puppet works with Vagrant to provision machines.

Understanding Puppet

Puppet is a configuration management tool that is used for deploying, configuring, and managing nodes (servers).

Puppet was released by Luke Kanies in 2005. It was written in C++, and Clojure and runs on Linux, Unix, and Windows. The current version is 5.5.3 and was released in July 2018. Puppet as a software falls into the infrastructure as code category, which means that you configure and make changes using code and configuration files. Puppet uses manifest files to help configure nodes/servers (we'll learn more about this in a later section).

Puppet uses a pull configuration (master and slave) architecture in which the nodes (Puppet agent) poll the master server for configuration files and changes. There is a four-step life cycle in this master/slave process:

1. The node sends facts about itself to the master server.
2. The master server uses these facts to compile a catalog as to how the node should be configured. It then sends the catalog back to the node.
3. The node uses the catalog to configure itself to the desired state, as described in the manifest file.
4. The node now sends a report to the master with any changes or errors. These reports can then be seen in the Puppet dashboard.

Puppet also supports a multi-master architecture to reduce downtime and offer high availability. When a master server falls over or faces any issues, another master server can take its place. Puppet agents will then poll this new master server for any configuration changes.

As part of the configuration process, there are multiple steps that Puppet takes to transform code in configuration files and configure a node into a desired state.

Resources

Puppet configuration often starts with a resource. You can think of a resource as code that describes the desired state of part of the node. This could be a specific package that needs to be installed such as nginx.

Manifest

A Puppet program is know as a manifest. A manifest contains Puppet configuration code and has the `.pp` file extension. These blocks of code are the resources that we spoke about in the previous section.

Compile

The compile process is when the Puppet master takes the manifest files and compiles them into a catalog. This catalog is then used by the nodes for provisioning and to reach the desired state.

Catalogs

A Puppet catalog is a document that has been created by the master server. It is created by compiling the Puppet manifest file. It can handle multiple manifest files, too. The catalog is then used by the node to set the desired system state.

Apply

If a node/server has a catalog, then it must apply that configuration to itself. This is the process of installing any necessary files, services, and software. It allows the node to reach the desired state.

Desired state

When speaking about Puppet and provisioning, you will hear about the *desired state*. In terms of Puppet, it simply means that the node/server has been completely provisioned and is now in the correct state. The software and services have been installed and are running correctly.

Puppet apply and Puppet agent

In this section, we will learn more about the two Puppet provisioning options available in Vagrant—`puppet apply` and `puppet agent`. In the following section, we will use both of these options to provision our own Vagrant machine.

Puppet apply

Using the Puppet apply option to provision a Vagrant machine allows you to use Puppet without the need for a Puppet master. It works by calling the `puppet apply` command on the guest machine. This can be useful for testing Puppet configurations if you do not have a Puppet master or you just need to get up and running quickly.

Options

There are 14 different options available when using Puppet apply in Vagrant. These options are to be applied in your Vagrantfile and can help give you more control over the Puppet provisioner:

- `binary_path`:

    Type: `string`

    Description: This is a path on the guest to the Puppet's bin directory.

- `facter`:

    Type: `hash`

    Description: This is a hash of available facter variables (also know as facts).

- `hiera_config_path`:

    Type: string

    Description: This is the path (on the host) to the hiera configuration.

- `manifest_file`:

    Type: `string`

    Description: This is the name of the manifest file that Puppet will use. The default is `default.pp`.

- `manifests_path`:

    Type: `string`

    Description: This is the path to the directory where the manifest files are. The default is `manifests`.

- `module_path`:

    Type: `string/array of strings`

    Description: This can be a path or paths to the directory (on the host) that contains any Puppet modules.

- environment:

    Type: string

    Description: This is the name of the Puppet environment.

- environment_path:

    Type: string

    Description: This is a path to the directory (on the host) which contains environment files.

- environment_variables:

    Type: hash

    Description: This is a set of environment variables (in a string of key/value pairs) which are to be used before Puppet apply runs.

- options:

    Type: array of strings

    Description: These are options that can be passed into the Puppet executable when Puppet is running.

- synced_folder_type:

    Type: string

    Description: This option allows you to specify what types of synced folder to use. This will use the synced folder type by default.

- synced_folder_args:

    Type: array

    Description: This is an array of arguments (values) that are passed to the folder sync. You can send specific arguments depending on the type of synced folder that you have chosen (see the preceding option).

- temp_dir:

    Type: string

    Description: This is the directory (on the guest machine) where any Puppet run data will be stored, such as manifest files.

- working_directory:

    Type: string

    Description: This is the working directory (on the guest machine) when Puppet is running.

Puppet agent

When using the Puppet agent to provision a Vagrant machine, you will need a Puppet master server to connect to. The master server will provide modules and manifests for the node to use. This provisioner works by using the puppet agent command, which is supplied by Puppet.

Options

There are seven different options available when using Puppet apply in Vagrant. These options are to be applied in your Vagrantfile and can help give you more control over the Puppet provisioner:

- binary_path:

    Type: string

    Description: This is a path on the guest to the Puppet's bin directory.

- client_cert_path:

    Type: string

    Description: This is the path to the client certificate for the node. The default value is nothing, which means that no client certificate will be uploaded.

- client_private_key_path:

    Type: string

    Description: This is the path to the client key for the node. The default value is nothing, which means that no client key will be uploaded.

- facter:

    Type: hash

    Description: This is a hash of available facter variables (also know as facts).

- options:

    Type: string/array

    Description: These are options that can be passed to Puppet when the puppet agent command is ran.

- puppet_node:

    Type: string

    Description: This is the name that you wish to give the node. If no value is set, then Vagrant will attempt to use the hostname (if set in the Vagrantfile) or fall back to the name of the box used.

- puppet_server:

    Type: string

    Description: This is the hostname of the Puppet server. If no value is set, then the default value will be set to puppet.

Puppet Manifest example and syntax

A manifest is a Puppet program. It is made up of code that tells Puppet what to do, such as executing commands, installing software, and running services. A manifest file or multiple manifest files are one of the main part(s) of a module. A manifest file uses the .pp file extension and can be found in the manifests folder.

There are various sections found in a manifest file, such as exec, package, service, and file. Let's dive into the syntax of a manifest file.

Syntax

The manifest file is taken up with declaring resources which can be grouped into classes. The manifest file uses a domain-specific language called Puppet, which is similar to YAML or Ruby (when writing a Vagrantfile).

Here is an example manifest that installs and runs the nginx web server. Let's create a new manifest and call it nginx.pp:

```
package { "nginx":
    ensure => installed
}

service { "nginx":
    require => Package["nginx"],
    ensure => running,
    enable => true
}
```

There are a few things to note in the preceding example. Each resource (section) starts with the category. We are using two categories – package and service. In a resource block, we wrap the values within curly parentheses, {}, and we then reference the name (nginx) and set the values we require.

There are a few keywords that we are using in the resource blocks – ensure, require, and enable. These keywords help describe what should happen for the node to reach a desired state. The ensure keyword is used to ensure that the package or service is doing what you want it to, such as installing or running. The require keyword is used when a specific resource relies on another resource. In the service resource, we are using the keyword enable, which allows us to specify if a service is active or not. It can be useful if you need to temporarily disable a service while testing.

You can add comments into the manifest file by using the hashtag/pound symbol. The following is an example:

```
# This comment wont be parsed by Puppet but it will be useful for other
developers/DevOps
```

Provisioning with Puppet

Let's get to the exciting part! We will now use Puppet apply and Puppet agent to provision a Vagrant machine. We'll look at both options and install the nginx web server. We'll configure it using the Vagrantfile as a base but also add in Puppet-specific configuration such as manifests.

Provisioning with Puppet apply

The Puppet apply provision option in Vagrant allows you to get up and running quickly with Puppet. You do not require a separate Puppet master server when using this option. Let's get started:

1. Create a new directory for this project and move into it.
2. Create a directory and call it manifests.
3. In the manifests folder, create a manifest file called nginx.pp. Inside this file, we'll insert the following instructions:

```
package { "nginx":
    ensure => installed
}
service { "nginx":
    require => Package["nginx"],
    ensure => running,
    enable => true
}
```

Let's break down this manifest file. First of all, we are executing the apt-get update command to update packages in Ubuntu. We then install the nginx package, which is started as a service. We ensure that it's running and enabled.

4. Back to Vagrant. Let's run the vagrant init -m command to create a minimal Vagrantfile.
5. Let's add some configuration into the Vagrantfile:

```
Vagrant.configure("2") do |config|
    config.vm.box = "ubuntu/xenial64"
    config.vm.network "private_network", ip: "11.11.11.11"
    config.vm.provision "shell", :inline => <<-SHELL
        apt-get update
        apt-get install -y puppet
    SHELL
    config.vm.provision "puppet" do |pup|
```

```
            pup.manifest_file = "nginx.pp"
      end
end
```

Let's break the Vagrantfile down. We first set the box to use Ubuntu Xenial 64 Bit, and then set the network to use a private network and a static IP address of 11.11.11.11. We need to install Puppet onto the guest machine, otherwise you will receive this error:

```
==> default: Running provisioner: puppet...
The `puppet` binary appears not to be in the PATH of the guest. This
could be because the PATH is not properly setup or perhaps Puppet is not
installed on this guest. Puppet provisioning can not continue without
Puppet properly installed.
```

To bypass this error, we are using the shell provisioner to first update the packages and then install the Puppet software on our Ubuntu box. Once this has completed, then the Puppet provisioner will begin. It will install and start running nginx:

```
==> default: Running provisioner: shell...
    default: Running: inline script
```

The preceding screenshot shows the shell provisioner. In the following screenshot, you can see the Puppet provisioner:

```
==> default: Running provisioner: puppet...
==> default: Running Puppet with nginx.pp...
==> default: Notice: Compiled catalog for ubuntu-xenial.home in environment prod
uction in 0.60 seconds
==> default: Notice: /Stage[main]/Main/Package[nginx]/ensure: ensure changed 'pu
rged' to 'present'
==> default: Notice: Finished catalog run in 5.67 seconds
```

6. Once complete, visit `http://11.11.11.11` in your browser, where you should see nginx's default page:

We can also check that Puppet is running on the Vagrant machine by SSH-ing in using the `vagrant ssh` command. Once in, run the `puppet help` command. We should see output similar to what's shown in the following screenshot:

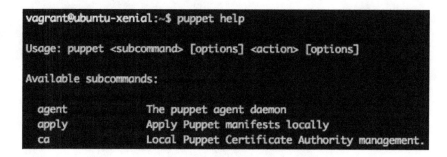

Congratulations! You have successfully provisioned a Vagrant machine using Puppet apply. You have created a Vagrantfile and a Puppet manifest file, installed nginx, and tested that the service is running correctly.

This is a fairly simple example, but Puppet is actually a very flexible and powerful provisioner. There is a lot you can do with Puppet and Vagrant. I would recommend that you experiment and learn more by testing out some of the options that are available.

Provisioning with Puppet agent

The second option when using Puppet as a provisioner is Puppet agent. Although this option has an added layer of complexity (the need for a Puppet master server), there is less configuration needed locally when it comes to Vagrant. We will not create a manifest file or any Puppet-related configuration on the host machine. It will all be handled by the Puppet master server.

The Puppet agent merely acts as a client which receives its commands from the server. In the following example, we are going to create a multi-machine setup that provisions Puppet master and Puppet agent machines:

1. Let's first create a new directory and move into that. I'm going to call mine `vagrant-puppet-agent` and use the following comments to create and move it:

   mkdir vagrant-puppet-agent && cd vagrant-puppet-agent

2. In our new directory, we can create a Vagrantfile by running the `vagrant init -m` command.

3. We now need to edit our Vagrantfile, which requires quite a bit of configuration. Not all of this is required for using the `puppet_server`/Puppet agent provision option, but we are also creating a Puppet master server:

```
Vagrant.configure("2") do |config|
    config.vm.box = "ubuntu/xenial64"
        # Puppet master configuration
        config.vm.define "puppetmaster" do |pm|

            pm.vm.provider "virtualbox" do |v|
                v.memory = 2048
                v.cpus = 2
            end

            pm.vm.network "private_network", ip:
"10.10.10.11"

            pm.vm.provision "shell", :inline => <<-SHELL
                sudo echo "10.10.10.11
master.example.com" | sudo tee -a /etc/hosts
                sudo echo "10.10.10.12
node.example.com" | sudo tee -a /etc/hosts
                wget
https://apt.puppetlabs.com/puppetlabs-release-pc1-xenial.deb
                sudo dpkg -i puppetlabs-release-pc1-
```

```
xenial.deb
                        sudo apt-get update -y
                        sudo apt-get install -y puppetserver
                        sudo awk '{sub(/-Xms2g -Xmx2g -
XX:MaxPermSize=256m/,"-Xms512m -Xmx512m")}1'
/etc/default/puppetserver > tmp.txt && mv tmp.txt
/etc/default/puppetserver
                        sudo echo "*" | sudo tee -a
/etc/puppetlabs/puppet/autosign.conf
                        sudo echo "autosign = true" | sudo tee
-a /etc/puppetlabs/puppet/puppet.conf
                        sudo echo
"certname=master.example.com" | sudo tee -a
/etc/puppetlabs/puppet/puppet.conf
                        sudo echo "[agent]" | sudo tee -a
/etc/puppetlabs/puppet/puppet.conf
                        sudo echo "certname=node.example.com"
| sudo tee -a /etc/puppetlabs/puppet/puppet.conf
                        sudo echo "exec { 'apt-get update':
path => '/usr/bin' } package { "nginx": ensure => installed }
service { "nginx": require => Package["nginx"], ensure =>
running, enable => true }" | sudo tee -a
/etc/puppetlabs/code/environments/production/manifests/default.
pp
                        sudo systemctl enable puppetserver
                        sudo systemctl start puppetserver
                SHELL
        end

        # Puppet Node configuration
        config.vm.define "pnode" do |pn|

                pn.vm.network "private_network", ip:
"10.10.10.12"

                pn.vm.provision "shell", :inline => <<-SHELL
                sudo echo "10.10.10.11 master.example.com" |
sudo tee -a /etc/hosts
                sudo echo "10.10.10.12 node.example.com" |
sudo tee -a /etc/hosts
                apt-get update
                apt-get install -y puppet
                sudo puppet agent --enable
                sudo echo "autosign = true" | sudo tee -a
/etc/puppet/puppet.conf
                sudo echo "certname=master.example.com" | sudo
tee -a /etc/puppet/puppet.conf
                sudo echo "[agent]" | sudo tee -a
```

```
/etc/puppet/puppet.conf
            sudo echo "certname=node.example.com" | sudo
tee -a /etc/puppet/puppet.conf
      SHELL

   pn.vm.provision "puppet_server" do |pup|
         pup.puppet_node = "nginxplease"
         pup.puppet_server = "master.example.com"
         pup.options = "--verbose --waitforcert 10"
   end

 end
end
```

This is the largest Vagrantfile we've created so far, but it covers a lot of configuration and it creats multiple Vagrant machines. Let's break it down:

1. We first set the box to use Ubuntu Xenial 64 Bit (this will apply to both machines as it's outside their configuration blocks).

2. Secondly, we define a `puppetmaster` block, which is used to configure the Puppet master machine. In this block, there is a large amount of custom configuration. Some of these parts are used to help suppress errors and may not always be needed. We need a powerful machine to meet the minimum requirements, so we will set the RAM memory and CPU count. We then create a shell provisioner, which installs the Puppet server software and makes various configuration changes to multiple files.

3. Thirdly, we define a `pnode` configuration block, which is used to configure the Puppet node/agent machine. We use the shell provisioner to install Puppet and make some configuration changes to multiple files. We also set the provisioner to use `puppet_server`, which is also known as Puppet agent. We set the node name, server host, and some additional options, which are to be sent to the command when Puppet is run.

4. Let's now run the `vagrant up --provision` command. This will take some time as it must first configure the Puppet master machine and then the Puppet agent machine.

   During the `up` process, you will see lots of out-put – mainly green, but some red, too. Don't worry too much about the red as it's not so much an error in our scenario as another level of output. Green is the output from the Vagrant machine, while red might be output from the Puppet master running within the Vagrant machine.

5. We'll first see the Puppet master provisioner begin. During this process, we'll also see the output from our `echo` statement, which is adding two records into the `/etc/hosts` file:

```
==> puppetmaster: Running provisioner: shell...
    puppetmaster: Running: inline script
    puppetmaster: 10.10.10.11 master.example.com
    puppetmaster: 10.10.10.12 node.example.com
```

Nearing the end of provisioning the Puppet master, we will see more output while we add additional information into the `puppet.conf` file. In red, we can see the Puppet master's output as it starts the service:

```
puppetmaster: *
puppetmaster: autosign = true
puppetmaster: certname=master.example.com
puppetmaster: [agent]
puppetmaster: certname=node.example.com
puppetmaster: exec { 'apt-get update': path => '/usr/bin' } package { nginx: ensure => installed } s
ervice { nginx: require => Package[nginx], ensure => running, enable => true }
    puppetmaster: Synchronizing state of puppetserver.service with SysV init with /lib/systemd/systemd-s
ysv-install...
    puppetmaster: Executing /lib/systemd/systemd-sysv-install enable puppetserver
```

6. We now start provisioning the second Vagrant machine, which is acting as our client/node in this example and using the Vagrant provision option for `puppet_server`. We'll see the node create and cache an SSL certificate:

```
==> pnode: Running provisioner: puppet_server...
==> pnode: Running Puppet agent...
==> pnode: Info: Creating a new SSL key for nginxplease
==> pnode: Info: Caching certificate for ca
==> pnode: Info: csr_attributes file loading from /etc/puppet/csr_attributes.yaml
==> pnode: Info: Creating a new SSL certificate request for nginxplease
==> pnode: Info: Certificate Request fingerprint (SHA256): DD:3A:33:B1:7D:61:5E:38:87:62:73:0C:83:23:E4:
AF:7B:0C:14:14:A4:B3:80:4C:9E:A2:D8:B4:B0:85:BC:D5
==> pnode: Info: Caching certificate for nginxplease
==> pnode: Info: Caching certificate_revocation_list for ca
==> pnode: Info: Caching certificate for ca
```

At the end of the node's provisioning, we will see it `retrieving` `pluginfacts` and then `applying configuration`. It will create a YAML file with the state and then it will use the catalog to reach a `desired state`. In the following screenshot, we can see that this was achieved in a swift 7.14 seconds:

```
==> pnode: Info: Retrieving pluginfacts
==> pnode: Info: Retrieving plugin
==> pnode: Info: Caching catalog for nginxplease
==> pnode: Info: Applying configuration version '1537564189'
==> pnode: Notice: /Stage[main]/Main/Package[nginx]/ensure: ensure changed 'purged' to 'present'
==> pnode: Notice: /Stage[main]/Main/Exec[apt-get update]/returns: executed successfully
==> pnode: Info: Creating state file /var/lib/puppet/state/state.yaml
==> pnode: Notice: Finished catalog run in 7.14 seconds
```

Now, let's check to make sure that our Puppet configuration has worked correctly and that we now have a node in the desired state (running nginx). Visit `http://10.10.10.12` in your browser. You should see nginx's default page:

We can also SSH into the machines individually to see their state. Run the `vagrant` `status` command to view each machine's status and their name (as we need this for the SSH command):

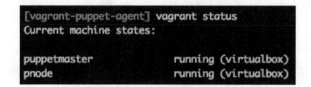

```
[vagrant-puppet-agent] vagrant status
Current machine states:

puppetmaster                    running (virtualbox)
pnode                           running (virtualbox)
```

Let's first SSH into the Puppet master by running the `vagrant ssh puppetmaster` command. Once in, run the `puppetserver --version` command to confirm that everything is running fine and to see what the current version is:

```
vagrant@ubuntu-xenial:~$ puppetserver --version
puppetserver version: 2.8.1
```

Let's now SSH into the Puppet node/agent by running the `vagrant ssh pnode` command. Once in, run the `puppet --version` command to confirm that everything is running fine and to see what the current version is:

```
vagrant@ubuntu-xenial:~$ puppet --version
3.8.5
```

If you wish to stop both machines, then run the `vagrant halt` command. By doing this, you can delete the machine states and any associated files by running the `vagrant destroy` command.

Congratulations! You have successfully provisioned a Vagrant machine using the Puppet agent option. We have created a traditional Puppet setup of the server and client by using the multi machine option in Vagrant, along with various provisioning and networking options.

Summary

In this chapter, we have learned all about Puppet and how to use it as a provisioner for Vagrant machines. We have also learned about the two supported provisioning methods of Puppet apply and Puppet agent.

In Chapter 14, *Salt - Using Salt to Provision a Vagrant Box*, we will focus on another provisioner supported by Vagrant. We'll learn about Salt and how it can be used to provision Vagrant machines. You'll get a good understanding of Salt as well as Salt states.

14
Salt - Using Salt to Provision a Vagrant Box

You've reached the final chapter of the book, and our provisioning miniseries. In this chapter, we'll learn more about the Salt provisioner that can be used with Vagrant. At the end of this chapter, you will have a good understanding of how to use Salt to provision Vagrant and know more about Salt as a standalone piece of configuration-management software. We'll learn about Salt and how it works.

Specifically, we'll cover the following topics:

- Understanding Salt
- Salt states
- The syntax of Salt states
- Provisioning a Vagrant machine with Salt
- Vagrantfile options available when using Salt

Understanding Salt

Salt is another member of the provisioning and infrastructure as code family. It can be compared directly to Chef, Ansible, and Puppet. It's written in the Python language and was first released in March 2011.

Salt can sometimes be referred to as the SaltStack platform. This is due to the modular approach in which the software has been designed and built. It's extensible, flexible approach allows you to add and remove modules.

Salt has one main setup—the client and server. You can think of it as a Puppet Master and Minion setup. Salt uses a server (Master) and client (Minion) for its configuration management. The other setup option that Salt supports is called **Masterless**,

Salt Master

A Salt Master is used to manage the infrastructure and the servers within it. It can run remote execution commands onto Minion servers and manage their state. It also can operate in a Master-tiered setup where commands can be passed down through lower Master servers. The Salt Master manages Salt Minions and is used to capture grains sent from the Minions. It can then use the grain data to decide how to manage that specific Minion. It runs a daemon called `salt-master`.

Salt Minion

A Salt Minion is a server/machine often controlled by the Salt Master. A Minion can run in a `masterless` setup too. A Salt Minion runs a daemon called `salt-minion` and its main purpose is to run commands sent from the Master, report data back, and send information about itself in the form of **grains**.

Modules

There are six different modules available in Salt. Each type of module offers a different action or function. We'll learn more about each here.

Execution

You can think of execution modules as `ad hoc` commands. These commands are run on the Minion (command line) machines/nodes. They are written using Python/Cython.

State

States are a core part of configuration management in Salt. A state is a file that configures and describes what state a machine should be in. This is very similar to the Puppet manifests that describe the desired state of the machine.

Grains

Grains are pieces of static information about the Minion. This information includes core details about the Minion, such as operating system, model, memory, and other data that is gathered and sent to the Master upon the initial connection. This can help the Master target different groups of Minions, such as targeting a specific operating system.

Renderer

A renderer in Salt is used to transform data types described in **SaLt State files (SLS)** into Python to be consumed and handled by Salt. A common example is an SLS file rendered into a Jinja template and then parsed as a YAML document. There are a few different combinations currently supported:

- Jinja and YAML
- Mako and YAML
- Wempy and YAML
- Jinja and JSON
- Mako and JSON
- Wempy and JSON

Returners

In Salt, a returner is used to handle and output from a command run on a Minion machine. The output/results data is always sent back to the Master but using a returner allows you to decide where that data goes. You can choose any service that can receive data, such as Redis or MySQL. This data can be used for analysis or archiving. It can give you better insights into what's happening on the Minions and which commands are performing best.

Runners

A Salt runner is very similar to an execution module. The one difference is that a runner is a command run and is executed on the Master server. A runner can be as simple or as complex as you like. They can be run using the `salt-run` command.

Salt states

Salt states are also known as state modules. They make up an important part of the state system used within Salt. A Salt state is used to describe what packages should be installed on the Minion and other options such as user accounts, running services, and folder permissions. We'll look at the Salt state syntax now.

Syntax and example

A Salt state file can often be found in the `roots` directory. It employs the `.sls` file extension and uses the **Yet Another Markup Language** (**YAML**) format for its contents. There is a certain hierarchy within a salt state file and that can go quite deep, depending on your requirements and configuration.

Let's break down an example Salt state file:

```
lampstack:
    pkg.installed:
        - pkgs:
        - mysql-server
        - php5
        - php-pear
        - php5-mysql
```

We first set a name for this section, in this example it's called `lampstack`. We then call `pkg.installed`, which verifies that certain packages have been installed. We use the - `pkgs` option and set the - `mysql-server`, - `php5`, - `php-pear`, and - `php5-mysql` values.

Provisioning Vagrant with Salt

Let's get to the main part of this chapter: provisioning a Vagrant machine with Salt. We'll look at the `masterless` configuration setup for this section. We'll learn how to install the Nginx web server onto our Vagrant machine:

1. Create a new folder/directory for this example. I'm calling mine `vagrant-salt`.
2. Move into the new folder and run the `vagrant init -m` command to create a new Vagrantfile.
3. We need to create some folders and files for Salt. Create a `roots` folder and a `minionfiles` folder. Inside the `roots` folder, create a file called `top.sls` and enter these contents:

```
base:
    '*':
        - base
```

Within the same folder (roots), create another file called base.sls and enter these contents:

```
nginx:
    pkg.installed:
        - name: nginx
```

The top file dictates what hosts to target. We can use the * icon here to indicate that we will target all hosts. This is not always the best option, but in this instance it will work fine. It also dictates what Salt file to use. The - base value translates into the base.sls file that we created.

The base.sls file is very minimal. It dictates that the nginx package (pkg) should be installed. Let's now move into the minionfile folder and create our base Minion file. Create the minion.yml file and enter the following contents:

```
master: localhost
file_client: local
```

Here we are setting the master value as localhost (as we are using a Masterless setup) and the file_client to local too. Save these files and return to the roots folder where the Vagrantfile is.

4. Set up the Vagrantfile. Edit the file to include these contents:

```
Vagrant.configure("2") do |config|
    config.vm.box = "ubuntu/xenial64"
    config.vm.network "private_network", ip: "10.10.10.20"
    config.vm.synced_folder "roots/", "/srv/salt"
    config.vm.provision :salt do |sa|
        sa.masterless = true
        sa.minion_config = "minionfiles/minion.yml"
        sa.run_highstate = true
    end
end
```

The Vagrantfile is fairly compact, but there are many options available to configure Salt. You'll learn more about these in the coming sections.

In this Vagrantfile, we first set the box to use Ubuntu Xenial 64 bit and we set a private network IP address as `10.10.10.20`. We then set up Vagrant's `synced_folder` option to share our roots folder with Salt so it can access our `top.sls` and `base.sls` files. In the next section, we set the provision block to use salt and set some basic values. We set the Masterless option to `true`, and the `minion_config` to use our recently created `minion.yml` file inside the `minionfiles` folder. We also set the `run_highstate` option to `true` to suppress any errors and run the files.

5. Save the Vagrantfile and run `vagrant up --provision` to start the Vagrant machine.
6. During the `vagrant up` process, we will see some new output as defined by the Vagrantfile and Salt options. We'll first see the folder syncing setup. In the following screenshot, we can see Vagrant's `/srv/salt` folder linking to `/roots` on the host machine:

```
default: /srv/salt => /Users/alexbraunton/Projects/vagrant-salt/roots
```

We'll then see the `Running provisioner: salt...` section, which will show any output from the Salt provisioner. We can see that Salt checks a number of things such as whether `salt-minion` is installed or outputs that `Salt successfully configured and installed!`.

Salt has been installed and the Salt state and minion files have been parsed and executed:

```
==> default: Running provisioner: salt...
Copying salt minion config to vm.
Checking if salt-minion is installed
salt-minion was not found.
Checking if salt-call is installed
salt-call was not found.
Bootstrapping Salt... (this may take a while)
Salt successfully configured and installed!
run_overstate set to false. Not running state.overstate.
Calling state.highstate... (this may take a while)
orchestrate is nil. Not running state.orchestrate.
```

Once this is complete and the Vagrant machine is running, open a web browser and visit the private network IP address we set in the Vagrantfile. Open `http://10.10.10.20` and you should see the default Nginx welcome page:

Congratulations! You have successfully provisioned a Vagrant machine using Salt. We have used the `sls` files to dictate that the Nginx package should be installed. There are many different options that you can experiment with here, especially using a Master and Minion configuration setup.

Salt options available within Vagrant

As Salt is essentially built into Vagrant, there are many options available. There are currently six different types of options available to manage in the Vagrantfile. These option types are:

- Install
- Minion
- Master
- Execute states
- Execute runners
- Output control

Let's break these option groups down to see what specific options are available to configure.

Install options

These are fairly generic options and are used to manage the installation of Salt. Here are the options available:

- `install_master`: If this option is set to `true`, it will install the `salt-master` daemon
- `no_minion`: If set to true, this options will not install the minion
- `install_syndic`: Dictates whether to install `salt-syndic`
- `install_type`: Dictates the installation channel when installing via package manager, such as stable, daily, or testing
- `install_args`: When using Git, you can specify additional args, such as branch or tag
- `always_install`: Dictates whether to install binaries, even if they are already detected
- `bootstrap_script`: This is the path to your custom boostrap sh script
- `bootstrap_options`: Additional options to path to your custom bootstrap `sh` script
- `version`: This dictates the version of the Minion to be installed
- `python_version`: This dictates the major Python version to be installed on the Minion

Minion options

These are minion-specific options. These are only really used when the `no_minion` option is set to true (the default value). Here are the options available:

- `minion_config`: The path to a custom minion config file
- `minion_key`: The path to your minion key
- `minion_id`: A unique identifier for a minion
- `minion_pub`: The path to your minion public key
- `grains_config`: The path to a custom grains file
- `masterless`: This will call `state.highstate` in local mode
- `minion_json_config`: This is valid JSON used to configure the salt minion
- `salt_call_args`: Additional arguments to pass to the `salt-call` command if provisioning with Masterless

Master options

These are master-specific options. These are only really used when the `install_master` option is set to true. Here are the options available:

- `master_config`: This is the path to the master config file
- `master_key`: This is the path to your master key
- `master_pub`: This is the path to your public key
- `seed_master`: This is used to upload keys to the master
- `master_json_config`: This is valid JSON used to configure the master minion
- `salt_args`: Additional arguments to pass to the 'salt' command if provisioning with Masterless

Execute states

There is only one option here to control state-execution during provisioning:

- `run_highstate`: Executes `state.highstate` on `vagrant up`

Execute runners

These options control runner execution during provisioning. These are the options available:

- `run_overstate`: Dictates whether `state.over` is run during `vagrant up`
- `orchestrations`: Dictates whether `state.orchestrate` is run during `vagrant up`

Output control

These options are used to control the output of state execution:

- `colorize`: This dictates whether the output is colorized
- `log_level`: The level of output, the default value is `debug`
- `verbose`: This dictates whether the output of salt commands are to be displayed

Vagrant cheat sheet

Through this chapter, I have shown you various tips and tricks when using Vagrant. It's always helpful to learn the correct way of doing something and, when comfortable, using faster methods that you may have picked up along the way. In this section, we will highlight some Vagrant shortcuts that I use and that I hope will help you.

Testing a Vagrantfile

When working with a Vagrantfile, large or small, it can be useful to test it as you write it. If writing a complex Vagrantfile, it can be useful to test certain sections as you add them, without writing the whole thing and getting errors.

Run the `vagrant validate` command to test your Vagrantfile without having to run `vagrant up` or go through the whole process.

Saving a snapshot

You can quickly and easily save a snapshot of your Vagrant machine and roll back to that at a later date/time. This can be useful for testing purposes, local versioning, and general usage.

Run the `vagrant snapshot save [options] [vm-name] [snapshot-save-name]` command. The final parameter is used to give the snapshot a name so you can revert back to it.

Status

Vagrant offers two status commands. One to view the status of the machine in your current working directory (if any), and one to view the status of all machines on your system.

Use the `vagrant status` or `vagrant global-status` commands.

Boxes

Boxes are a big part of the Vagrant ecosystem and can sometimes be a pain to manage. Here are a few commands to help:

- Use `vagrant box list` to view all installed boxes on your system
- Use `vagrant box outdated --global` to check for updates on installed boxes
- Use `vagrant box prune` to remove old box versions

Hardware specification

If you need a more powerful Vagrant machine, you can use provider-specific code in your Vagrantfile to beef up the hardware spec. In the following example we will use the `memory` value to set a higher memory (RAM) for the machine. We also set the `cpus` value to set a higher processor count. Finally, we set the `gui` value so we can access the machine via a graphical user interface:

```
config.vm.provider "virtualbox" do |vb|
    vb.memory = 4096
    vb.cpus = 2
    vb.gui = true
end
```

This is VirtualBox-specific code.

Please note: You cannot specify a higher hardware specification than the host machine.

Code deployment

You can deploy code from Vagrant by running the vagrant push command. You will need to do some configuration first but this can be a good way of managing code and a machine at the same time. You will need to specify a remote server (such as FTP) in your Vagrantfile before running the command. Here is an example block:

```
config.push.define "ftp" do |push|
    push.host = "ftp.yourdeploymentexample.com"
    push.username = "yourftpusername"
    push.password = "yourftppassword"
end
```

You can use FTP, SFTP (by setting the secure option to true in the FTP version), Heroku, or execute commands that you have created for pushing code.

Multi-machine

Using Vagrant's multi-machine is a powerful and easy way to create an infrastructure. This can be used for testing or to closely replicate your production environment. You can set up multiple Vagrant machines in one Vagrantfile and then manage them separately.

Each machine gets its own block in the Vagrantfile so any options are specific to that one machine. You can use different provisioners, hardware specs, and other options in each block.

General

We've covered some specific parts, but it can be worth revisiting the basics when trying to solve a problem or learn more about specific features.

You can run the vagrant help command to list all commands in the system, which shows a description and usage. To get more information on a specific command, you can run the vagant [command-name] -h command.

The official Vagrant website and documentation is well written, easy to understand, and easy to use. I often refer to it when using something new or something I haven't used for a while.

Error messages in Vagrant are generally helpful and describe the error in a fairly easy-to-understand manner. If you have any issues, try to work through the error message. I often use search engines to find out how to fix an error.

Summary

In this chapter, we learned how to provision a Vagrant machine using the Salt software. We learned about the options available when configuring Salt with Vagrant, and looked at what Salt states are and their syntax.

The end of this chapter marks the end of our provisioning miniseries and the end of this book. I encourage you to keep exploring Vagrant and its many different features. We've focused mainly on provisioning in this book, but you could also look at the provider option in Vagrant. This allows you to manage which software actually powers the virtual machine. We use VirtualBox in this book, but there are other options, such as VMWare and Docker. It all depends on your environment and available software, but Vagrant can be flexible and will often meet your requirements.

Other Book You May Enjoy

If you enjoyed this book, you may be interested in these other books by Packt:

Hands-On Security in DevOps
Tony Hsu

ISBN: 978-1-78899-550-4

- Understand DevSecOps culture and organization
- Learn security requirements, management, and metrics
- Secure your architecture design by looking at threat modeling, coding tools and practices
- Handle most common security issues and explore black and white-box testing tools and practices
- Work with security monitoring toolkits and online fraud detection rules
- Explore GDPR and PII handling case studies to understand the DevSecOps lifecycle

DevOps with Kubernetes

Hideto Saito, Hui-Chuan Chloe Lee, Cheng-Yang Wu

ISBN: 978-1-78839-664-6

- Learn fundamental and advanced DevOps skills and tools
- Get a comprehensive understanding for container
- Learn how to move your application to container world
- Learn how to manipulate your application by Kubernetes
- Learn how to work with Kubernetes in popular public cloud
- Improve time to market with Kubernetes and Continuous Delivery
- Learn how to monitor, log, and troubleshoot your application with Kubernetes

Leave a review - let other readers know what you think

Please share your thoughts on this book with others by leaving a review on the site that you bought it from. If you purchased the book from Amazon, please leave us an honest review on this book's Amazon page. This is vital so that other potential readers can see and use your unbiased opinion to make purchasing decisions, we can understand what our customers think about our products, and our authors can see your feedback on the title that they have worked with Packt to create. It will only take a few minutes of your time, but is valuable to other potential customers, our authors, and Packt. Thank you!

Index